INCREASING YOUR PERSONAL
AND PROFESSIONAL EFFECTIVENESS

A Manual for Women Who Want to Accomplish

More Without Changing Who They Are

INCREASING YOUR PERSONAL
AND PROFESSIONAL EFFECTIVENESS

A Manual for Women Who Want to Accomplish

More Without Changing Who They Are

By Dixie L. Benshoff, Ph.D., Psychologist

Edited by Stacey R. Schneider, Pharm D

API
Ajoyin Publishing, Inc.
P.O. 342
Three Rivers, MI 49093
www.ajoyin.com

Please direct your inquiries to admin@ajoyin.com

ISBN: 9781609201210

Printed in the United States of America.

TABLE OF CONTENTS

DEDICATION

THIS BOOK IS DEDICATED TO all the women who went before, and to all the women who strive every day to "do the right thing" in their personal and professional relationships and still worry that they could have done more.

And to my mother who taught me to have the courage to want what I want, to expect that I can achieve it, and to attempt to remove barriers that might block my way without changing who I was.

And to my father who taught me not to confuse obstinacy with courage.

And finally, to Tangelo, my ever-constant feline companion, whom I lost in November of 2015. I finished it, buddy! Thanks for your help.

ACKNOWLEDGEMENTS

I HOPE, DEAR READER, THAT you do not skip this page. While you may assume that this page is not important, it is arguably the most important page in this book. For it is this page where the author humbles herself and admits that this book would not have been written without the personal and professional efforts of others. Please indulge me and if you do, I promise to make the rest of the book "readable" and "useful."

This is the third iteration of this book. With each telling, formatting changes were made and errors needed to be corrected. Morgan L. Brown stepped in at a moment's notice and proved not only to be a capable copy editor, but a tactful and knowledgeable communicator. Without her efforts this book would not be as clear or as presentable to you.

I want to thank Vi McCarty whose skills and talent for typing I have depended on since we worked together on our high school newspaper many years ago. Thanks to Diane Grogan who started this process but had to stop due to family obligations. To Becky Davis, a big thank you for your administrative assistance for over thirty years. To my editor, Stacey Schneider, who not only typed the narrative that I scribbled, but tactfully corrected my mistakes, and stroked my ego when I was discouraged. Sincere gratitude goes to the talented artist, Jeanne Carr, who did the cover. To her I say… A picture may speak a thousand words, but your drawings leave me speechless. Thank you Pam Eichorn of Ajoyin who made it exactly that. She went out of her way to smooth the rough edges, and make this process a joyful one instead of (what could have been) a frustrating one.

Drs. Russell Getson, Richard Rynearson, Suzanne Hetrick, and Robert Byrnes all took a chance on a young student and/or psychologist and lent their time and talent to train her and encourage her. I'll never forget your lessons and I remain appreciative of your leadership.

Of course, it would not be possible if my dear friend and mentor, Nancy Gabalac, had not joined me and supported me in developing this curriculum and co-teaching the content. I must thank my professional and personal friends Dr. Denise Gibson and Dr. Claire Draucker who challenged me intellectually and who have always "had my back." Sisterhood is powerful!

A sincere expression of gratitude goes to Dr. Holly Gerzina for organizing the women's seminars and Dr. Janice MacKichan for underwriting them.

Without the support of my husband, Tim Ludick, and son, David Ludick, I would not have had the time or the "gumption" to make the sacrifices necessary to complete this project. They tirelessly listened, edited, commented, and encouraged, and in so doing provided insight and perception.

Finally, to all of the women who have attended my seminars and told me your stories, thank you so much! I hope I have done you justice.

FOREWORD...

I WAS SO EXCITED I could barely contain myself. At the ripe old age of five, I had been selected to lead the kindergarten rhythm band before the entire PTA! We practiced and practiced. The entire class had been assembled just the way a real orchestra was, with triangles in one section, maracas in another section, tambourines by themselves, and sticks across the back. They corresponded loosely to the brass, strings and woodwind sections of the world famous Cleveland Orchestra which we had visited on a recent field trip. I had been selected to be the conductor because, according to the music teacher, I had a natural sense of rhythm and I was good at mimicking. So when we returned from our field trip I had the movements of the conductor down. Mrs. Schaffer, our teacher, appreciated my diligence and accuracy, and the music teacher said that I had a natural sense of rhythm. I had been selected to lead the band! With pride I told my parents the good news and they applauded. Mom looked a little worried, which I did not quite understand. (She knew I wasn't shy.) In the week that followed, I discovered why.

"Dixie," my kindergarten teacher said. "I am sorry to have to tell you this, but you cannot be the conductor for the orchestra." She continued, "You see, Dixie, only boys can be orchestra conductors and we have selected one of your male classmates. We would like you to continue to rehearse because you do have a strong sense of rhythm and you are very comfortable in front of the audience, but after all, girls cannot be conductors."

And so it began...

Several other events unfolded before I achieved my Ph.D. at the age of 27 in 1977 – one of a few females in my cohort to do so. When I registered for the college track in high school with thoughts of maybe becoming a doctor, the guidance counselor gently told me that ladies cannot be doctors and I would automatically be entered into the business track so I could be a secretary. If I insisted on college I could be a teacher or I could go to nursing school. My mother, who had lost the conductor issue years earlier, was now before the school board insisting on college preparatory classes for me. The administrators agreed that indeed I must be reasonably bright, because I was quick at alphabetizing. They assured my mother I would be offered a fine position at the telephone company as an operator.

My mother was adamant. She knew what discrimination felt like. She herself had been valedictorian of her high school class. When she was offered a full scholarship to the local college her dad yelled, "That ain't meant for women," and she was forbidden to attend. My mother taught me that I should assert my rights politely but effectively. I should never accept being held back because I was female. I did indeed get into those college preparatory classes.

In undergraduate school, I majored in English with a concentration in journalism. During the summer and after graduation, I worked at the local newspaper. I won a national award for feature writing but was told that women were assigned to the society page. After writing stories that sounded like this… *Looking lovely in her pink chiffon, Mrs. Migillicuddy poured from a Waterford crystal punch bowl handed down from her grandmother,* I knew it was time to look for something else. I was intrigued with law and politics, but soon discovered that in the seventies women who had their juris doctorate could work in a law office but could not necessarily practice law – just because they were women. I was a certified teacher, but I knew I wanted to go into a helping profession and went back to graduate school. I wanted to be a guidance counselor to help the high school students that I taught. Once I was admitted to the guidance department a mentor (male) said to me, "I think you are very skillful. I would like to see you pursue a Ph.D. in psychology." At that time there were only a few women in the clinical psychology department. So I minored in clinical psychology and majored in counseling.

Did all of these experiences color my approach to this book? Of course they did! They would have to. Our experiences contribute to who we are. Nonetheless the skills that I present in this book are useful to both men and women. It's just that women versus men sometimes seem to be more concerned about how they are perceived — or maybe just more comfortable articulating that fact. Nevertheless, I hope this book reaches both men and women who want to become more personally and professionally effective. Whether that is because they are denied their rights like my mother was or they simply want to be better at what they do or who they are. As for my thwarted aspirations to lead a rhythm band? It's never too late to discover who you are. My son just bought me my own set of Ludwigs.

PART ONE
THE FUNDAMENTALS

CHAPTER 1

The Spirits of the Staircase

THE QUEASY STOMACH, THE DISTURBED sleep, the countless hours of rumination are all familiar signs of anxiety and dread. Sometimes these feelings occur because we neglect to take action when conflict arises or the action we nearly all of us performed was impulsive and ineffective. Our protective mind attempts to impose systematic organization on our own perception of chaos by replaying the scene and thinking negative thoughts about the way we conducted ourselves. I am talking about a phenomena experienced by nearly all of us, arguably experienced more by working women. This is what I mean. You are a woman balancing the responsibility of your job and your home. You have just left a conflictual situation at work. Perhaps it was a conversation with a coworker, perhaps it was a meeting with your boss, maybe it was a committee or group meeting, but you leave the situation feeling uncomfortable, anxious, and maybe even angry. That night after you have performed the duties of your "second shift," whether that is fixing dinner, helping with homework, or starting laundry, you settle in to discuss the situation with your partner. For some of you this will bring needed relief. For many others this will leave you as frustrated as you were before. As you toss and turn trying desperately to fall asleep, you are bothered by recurrent thoughts such as *I should have said this* or *I wish I could have handled myself like...*fill in the blank with the name of someone you admire. This attempt to replay the conflictual scenario and insert an empowering response is our way of feeling more in control of the situation that elicited feelings of helplessness and inadequacy.

The phenomenon described above is so universal that the French actually have a name for it. It is called *L'esprit d'escalier* translated literally as the "The Spirit of the Staircase." Figuratively, it means that the person who climbs the stairs at night readying her or himself for bed is haunted by the spirits of the staircase that murmur... *You could have said this* or *You should have done that.*

The purpose of this book is to exorcise those spirits. I believe we each have the power to control our own behavior. Once you are given the resources you can choose behavior that can position you so that you are not haunted by the ghosts who paralyze you with fear and a loss of self-respect. It is not enough to simply tell ourselves we have the power to change our destiny. We must also master the skills necessary. Nothing improves self-esteem like success. In order to handle conflictual situations more confidently, we have to believe that we can, and in order to believe that we can we have to possess the skills that set us up for success. Conversely, if we have self-doubt we don't take risks. If we don't take risks we continue to behave in a way that becomes habitual for us. If those habits are successful then we gain self-respect and increase our self-esteem. If they are not successful we lose self-respect and so begins the vicious cycle. Make no mistake, I am not suggesting that we are unsuccessful people not worthy of respect when we are bothered by conflict. However, I am suggesting that certain situations or certain people stimulate a response from within us. This response frequently leaves us feeling unsettled or questioning our own value and effectiveness. This book is designed to address your feelings, and increase your belief and ability to handle these situations so that you are no longer haunted by the spirits of the staircase. At the end of each chapter, I offer a take home message or summary which provides the steps necessary to chase away the spirits of discontentment and doubts.

Take home message: People in general, but women in particular, can worry about a situation and question themselves in the process. This tendency can erode self-confidence and effect future behavior. Women are especially vulnerable because they tend to be external validators. That is, they seek validation in terms of what others think, rather than internal validators who believe that self-sufficiency and independence is more valuable than pleasing others.

CHAPTER 2

The Set Up

IN THE FALL OF 2014, I agreed to explore this theory with a group of professional women who held positions of great responsibility at an institution that commanded great respect, partially because of its mission, and partially because of its well-deserved reputation. Along the way, other colleagues have made contributions to this book as well, but the initial inspiration came from this intimate group of professional women. These women were very accomplished in their fields and deserving of respect in their own right, yet each confessed that something was missing. Unable to articulate what that was, they came to believe that they craved validation that could only be achieved through power.

Not the power that is created with wealth, status, or position, rather, the power that is enjoyed by someone who is quietly confident with her own ability to handle conflict, turmoil, and chaos inherent in the daily routine of a woman who has great responsibility in her professional position as well as great expectations in her personal relationships. This book is the manual for acquiring and keeping that power. This book is the professional woman's manual for increasing her personal and professional effectiveness. It is a guide for the woman who wants to accomplish more without changing who she is.

Each woman who shared her story presented a dilemma that caused her to be haunted. Oftentimes, she was unable to fully articulate what she could have done or said differently that would have resulted in her feeling satisfied. She instead felt belittled or, at best, uncomfortable. The only criteria for women submitting stories to this book was that the interpersonal exchange "haunted her." In other words, thinking about the interaction caused her to feel helpless and lose some self-respect, or at the very least, question her effectiveness.

Sections of this book will contain real-life scenarios offered by the women who participated in this seminar and in others given thereafter. I will describe the tenant of personal power. Then the story will be told by the person who offered it. An analysis will follow resulting in a co-offering of a skill, technique, or personal approach that could have impacted the outcome and chased away the spirits of the staircase.

The author wishes to remind the reader that names of people, places, relationships and titles have been changed to preserve anonymity. Any resemblance to actual people or events is purely coincidental.

In order to move to the skill-building phase, we must first adopt a certain belief system. The beliefs discussed in this book are as follows:

1. All behaviors can be placed on a continuum and we as individuals can move up and down the continuum choosing behavior that will be in our best interest.
2. The primary purpose of any personal interaction is not necessarily the content being discussed. In fact, it seldom is. The primary purpose of any human interaction is to leave the interaction feeling okay about ourselves and the way we handled the interaction.
3. We are in control of our behavior and we always have choices.
4. Freedom of choice facilitates acquisition of power.
5. Irrational beliefs impede our ability to choose behavior that will be in our best interest.
6. Choosing to share power invariably increases power.

In the final chapter, I will discuss how women are in a position to affect the power differential through competence, compassion, and confidence. To put it in the vernacular, women need to be savvy, sassy, and strong. In order for women to be credible, they have to display competence, but they must also be approachable and warm. Linguistic literature suggests that women are generally associated with descriptors such as nurturing, supportive, and caring. Men are associated with descriptors such as strong, powerful, and arrogant. The implication is male leaders with competence are seen as strong and powerful and must guard against being seen as arrogant if they desire likeability. On the contrary, female leaders have to guard against being seen as "soft." If they overcompensate by becoming abrasive, they run the risk of being disliked. Observers tend not to respect women they do not like. If women do not want this distraction, they need to put effort into being warm and approachable to gain respect. Being competent is not enough. Is this fair? Certainly not. Is this reality? I believe it is.

This may sound contradictory to say do not change who you are but learn to be likeable and approachable. Learn what it is about you that is already effective and learn what has become habitual and does not serve your best interests. Your personal and professional goals for effectiveness might very well be a desire to get to the top, but it also may be choosing to stay where you are. Choosing to stay, rather than believing it to be foisted upon you, makes all the difference in the world. It ensures that you will not be haunted by the spirits of the staircase. The purpose of our interaction is not to get our own way — that is secondary. The primary goal of interactions is for you to leave feeling confident about the way you handled the situation and ultimately to feel at peace with yourself. Let me repeat... The primary goal is to leave a potentially conflictual situation feeling confident about the way you handled yourself. I am reminded of the poem *Invictus,* which means unconquered, written when the author was very young. Himself an amputee, he wrote about the indefatigable human spirit.

Invictus

Out of the night that covers me,
Black as the pit from pole to pole,
I thank whatever gods may be
For my unconquerable soul.

In the fell clutch of circumstance
I have not winced nor cried aloud.
Under the bludgeonings of change
My head is bloody, but unbowed.

Beyond this place of wrath and tears
Looms but the horror of the shade,
Any yet the menace of the years
Finds, and shall find, me unafraid.

It matters not how strait the gate,
How charged with punishments the scroll.
I am the master of my fate;
I am the captain of my soul.

William Ernest Henley

Take home message: You can be in charge of your life by building a set of skills that will increase your competence and confidence. Even if you don't achieve the desired outcome, you will believe that you did all that you could rather than worry that you should have done more.

CHAPTER 3

The Frame of Reference

I FEEL AS THOUGH THIS disclaimer is in order. I do not sell these skills as if they are snake oil or a magic elixir. Instead I submit that by learning a few interpersonal communication skills you can take control of your life, reduce your symptoms of anxiety and depression, and increase the probability that you will be more self-confident, self-respectful, and ultimately happier. Now, I do not claim these ideas are original. I have practiced psychology for well over 30 years and I am thankful for my training and experience. I am a clinician who has treated thousands of patients. I am not a researcher and I am not writing this as an academician. I am certain that I will offer an idea, use a term, or refer to a psychological construct that was originated by someone else. After you have practiced for as long as I have this is highly likely. I can only hope that this book will serve as a respectful compilation of useful ideas that have been reported by others. By assimilating them into one workbook, I hope to give the reader tools that will facilitate confidence and mitigate self-regret. In order to accomplish this let's revisit the belief system we discussed in Chapter 2.

1. All behaviors can be placed on a continuum and we as individuals can move up and down the continuum choosing behavior that will be in our best interest.

If you promise not to tell my more learned psychological colleagues, I have decided to reduce all human behaviors to very simplistic terms. Those terms are passive, aggressive, and assertive. Refer to Table 1 to see a brief description of each behavioral type. These behaviors are on a continuum like this:

Passive   Assertive   Aggressive

Where do you think you fall on this continuum? Mark an X at that point. Place the X where your behavior falls most of the time. What if I asked you to draw a continuum for the way you are at work and the way you are at home? Would your marks be in different places? Chances are they might be. It's not unusual for women to be more aggressive at work and more passive at home or vice versa. A note of caution, this does not mean that you are a passive person or an aggressive person. It means that we engage in behavior patterns in certain environments or with specific people that predict that we will have a tendency to cluster our behaviors more consistently at one point or another on this continuum. For example, I once had a very powerful attorney tell me that she had no trouble being aggressive in her role as a prosecutor, but at home with her kids she described herself as a pushover easily manipulated by them due to her passive behavior.

Table 1. Differentiating Passive, Assertive, and Aggressive Behavior

Passive	Assertive	Aggressive
Allow others to make choices for you	You make your own choices	You make choices for yourself and others
Refuse to take responsibility for your own needs	Accept responsibility for your own needs	Put your own needs first, often disregarding the needs of others

Passive-aggressive behavior is a fourth behavioral type that is many times not easy to identify. Passive-aggressive behavior is exactly that. The perpetrator professes to be innocent however there is hostility or a veiled attempt at being aggressive. Behavior such as sarcasm, whining, and manipulation all belong in this category. Passive-aggressive people tend to express their negative feelings in an indirect manner, rather than stating their disapproval directly to the person concerned. There tends to be a great deal of hostility derived from miscommunication, failure to communicate, or the assumption that the other person knows what they are thinking or feeling. From a relationship perspective, this type of behavior can be the most difficult communication style to deal with since you are never quite sure what you are dealing with.

Most people have a tendency to think of themselves as one behavioral type or another. People move along the spectrum frequently and it is in their best interest to do so. Before you can gain the skill of being able to choose where you want to be on the continuum, you have to first identify what behaviors others display. In other words, where are they on the spectrum?

To acquire these skills let's practice.

1. Write down all of the behaviors that you would consider to be passive behaviors.

_____
_____
_____
_____
_____

2. Write down all of the behaviors that you would consider to be aggressive behaviors.

_____
_____
_____
_____
_____

3. Write down all of the behaviors that you would consider to be assertive behaviors.

_____
_____
_____
_____
_____

4. Write down all of the behaviors that you would consider to be passive-aggressive behaviors.

_____
_____
_____
_____

If you are like most people, you have not written anything so far. You have decided to skip ahead in the book to see if this exercise is worth your time. Congratulations! You have successfully listed the first behavior-avoidance, and that would go under passive. So would withdrawal, denial, deference, complacence, and acquiescence. All of those are behaviors we associate with passive behavior. Behaviors that you may have listed under aggressive behavior are flamboyant, loud, pushy, bossy, controlling, or intimidating. If you have a tendency to choose passive behavior most frequently you will not have as much difficulty listing the aggressive behavior. Conversely, if you are aggressive by nature you will experience disdain or disgust when you list the passive behaviors. People who have a tendency to choose passive behaviors most frequently are described as mousey, wimpy, sweet, shy, or nice. People who display aggressive behaviors most frequently are described as controlling, bossy, go-getters, confident, or abrasive. If you are like most people, your list under assertive will be more difficult for you to describe. Words such as confident, competent, and caring are most frequently associated with this type of behavior. Note: This is based on an association exercise given to classes of students over the last 20 years.

Unlike other books that contend you should always behave assertively, this book points out that there are times when it is in your best interest to be passive, aggressive, passive-aggressive, or assertive. Knowing when to choose behaviors from the continuum puts you in a position of personal power. In other words, I do not put a value judgment on any of these behaviors. For example, if you are asked to pull to the side of the road by a police officer, I suggest you become deferential and acquiescent. This is in your best interest. If you have consistently attempted to be assertive with someone who is aggressive and abrasive, I suggest you move up the continuum to confront that aggression with equal aggression. If you find yourself in a position where someone has power over you and there would be great personal costs/consequences to being passive or aggressive, you might choose to purposely be passive-aggressive. More about this later in the book.

Buying into this philosophy may be difficult for some people and certainly there are gender differences. We tend to associate males with aggression and females with passivity. When we encounter a female who is behaving consistently aggressively, we have a colorful slang term for her that begins with a "B." When we encounter a male that tends to be aggressive we have a colorful slang term for him that begins with the letter "P." However, the connotation is (wink, wink, nudge, nudge) that he is a force to be reckoned with and likely to be in a leadership position. A woman in this same situation might be viewed as unpleasant and abrasive and therefore overlooked for a promotion. Choosing to be assertive is gender neutral. I submit to you that if you consistently choose any of the other three behaviors then you run the risk of being perceived as lacking self-respect (passive), thinking too much of yourself or being arrogant (aggressive), or being manipulative (passive-aggressive). Behavior that tends to foster mutual self-respect is assertive behavior. The reason I describe it as mutual is because this is the behavior that will increase the probability of chasing away the spirits of the staircase.

For example, in my seminars, participants tend to report that when they are with someone who is behaving in a passive fashion saying consistently... *I don't care* or *whatever you want to do*, or saying nothing at all, they have the tendency to become frustrated with the passive person. They perceive them as being dependent and eventually become resentful of being cast in the role of making all the decisions. This flabbergasts the passive person who reports they are simply trying to get along and please the other person or "go with the flow" and be easy-going and cooperative.

When people are in the presence of individuals who are very comfortable with being aggressive they have a tendency to report that they typically become passive themselves and feel hurt and afraid. If they are so inclined they may become aggressive and retaliate (which is a more typical response for men). Women are more comfortable being passive-aggressive such as saying nothing at the time and then not following through on the directive issued by the bully or completing the request assigned by the aggressive boss then complaining to co-workers about his behavior. An assertive response, as we will see in the next few chapters, would be to address undesirable behavior in a respectful way that increases the probability that the aggressive person will think twice before aggressing against you again. More importantly, this will leave you with a sense of confidence and self-respect.

Here are the main differences between the behavioral types. If you choose passive behavior, you allow others to make the decisions and choices for you, and you give others the responsibility to meet your needs. If you choose passive-aggressive behavior, you are getting your own needs met, and you are making decisions for other people. By being emotionally dishonest you appear to lose but in reality you win. If you choose aggressive behavior, you get your own needs met regardless of the needs of others. You not only take responsibility for making your own decisions, but you also make decisions for other people. If you choose assertive behavior, you let others know in a calm and respectful way what your needs are and you ask others to help meet those needs. At the same time, you recognize the needs of others and you negotiate a solution that is agreeable even if those needs are in direct opposition. Ultimately, you take the responsibility for meeting your own needs.

This leads us to belief number two.

2. The primary purpose of any personal interaction is not necessarily the content being discussed. In fact, it seldom is. The primary purpose of any human interaction is to leave the interaction feeling okay about yourself and the way you handled the interaction.

Certainly, people find themselves in poverty, poor health, and in circumstances that seem beyond their control. But for every "bad card" dealt to the individuals in these unfortunate positions, there is almost always something that can be done to improve the situation, if only slightly. When there is not an alternative, say in the case of poor health, the ability to exert some sort of control over the potential treatment increases the likelihood that people will feel a greater sense of contentment and dignity.

In the article, "Heart Disease and Lifestyle: Why are Doctors in Denial?", Dr. John Mandrola writes, "I believe the collective denial of lifestyle disease is the reason why cardiology is in an innovation rut. The denial is not active or overt. It is indolent and apathetic. Bulging waistlines, thick necks, sagging muscles, and waddling gaits have begun to look like normal. During the electronic medical record click-fest after seeing a patient, I rarely click on 'normal' physical exam. The general appearance is abnormal — either overweight or obese. In mathematics, an asymptote is a line that approaches a given curve but does not meet it at a finite distance. This is how I see modern cardiology. Our tricks can no longer overcome eating too much and moving too little. We approach health but never get there. If you waddle, snore at night, and cannot see your toes while standing, how much will a statin or ACE inhibitor or even LCZ696 help?"[1]

The point he is trying to make is exactly the same as mine — it is our choice of behavior which predicts success and ultimately happiness in life. Individuals who believe ... *I have a bad heart or I have diabetes therefore I cannot…* (fill in the blank) are overlooking the fact that they are indeed in charge of their own health which includes proper diet, exercise, and so on. They can make a positive impact on the outcome. The same is true on interpersonal relationships. By choosing the "healthiest" of choices more often than not we can come to believe in ourselves and increase our self-confidence. By doing so we increase our self-esteem. By doing so we increase our ability to take risks. By doing so we have a richer, fuller life with a greater chance for success and happiness.

Most people make the mistaken assumption that they are assertive. They will describe themselves as assertive when in reality they are actually aggressive. It is quite difficult to describe assertive behavior and perhaps even more difficult to maintain assertive behavior. The following table compares the different behavioral styles. If you are not sure how you are behaving or how others are behaving towards you, identify any of the characteristics on this matrix. For example, if you know you are feeling misunderstood, perhaps you are being passive-aggressive. If you know you are feeling guilty, perhaps you are being aggressive. If you are feeling confident or accomplished then chances are you are being assertive.

Comparison of Alternative Behavior Styles

Passsive-aggressive	Passsive	Assertive	Aggressive
Action: Hides reaction	Action: Underreacts	Action: Acts	Action: Overreacts
You feel self-righteous	You feel anxious, ignored, helpless, manipulated	You feel confident, self-respectable, goal oriented	You feel superior and powerful
Later you feel misunderstood	Later you feel angry at self or others	Later you feel accomplished	Later you feel guilty
Others feel they have been taken by you or angry	Others feel superior, guilty, or frustrated	Others feel valued and respected	Others feel angry, afraid, hurt
Others view you as dishonest or sneaky	Others view you as flighty	Others view you as honest and confident	Others view you as oboxious and controlling
Outcome: You may get what you want but at other's expense	Outcome: Others get what they want at your expense	Outcome: You may get what you want while everyone's rights are respected	Outcome: You get what you want at other's expense and your rights are upheld while others are violated

Before venturing on in this book, think about the descriptions of each behavior. Spend the next few days just simply observing yourself and others. This will help you begin to be able to identify when you are behaving in a passive-aggressive, passive, aggressive, or assertive way. If you are unable to identify these behaviors within yourself, see if you can identify them in other people. After some careful observation move on to the next chapter to complete the worksheets.

Take home message: The more you practice, the quicker you will be able to identify behavior in yourself and others. The quicker you are, the better able you will be to choose the behavior that will increase the probability that you will not be haunted by the spirits of the staircase, ultimately leaving the situation feeling ok with the behavior you chose.

References

1. Mandrola, J. Heart Disease and Lifestyle: Why Are Doctors in Denial? *Medscape.* Jan 12, 2015.

CHAPTER 4

The Meat and Potatoes

Now THAT YOU HAVE SPENT some time observing your behavior and the behavior of other people around you, complete the set of exercises below.

Passive Behavior

If I chose passive behavior I:

- Allowed others to make decisions and choices for me
- Gave others the responsibility for meeting my needs
- Never wanted to make the other party uncomfortable

I chose passive behavior when I (list examples):

1.
2.
3.

I chose passive behavior most during this week when I was dealing with people (circle one):

1. At work
2. In my family
3. Who are close friends
4. In social situations
5. Who were strangers
6. Other

I am dissatisfied with the way I dealt with _____

because_____

If I could do it differently, I might _____

Passive-Aggressive Behavior

If I chose passive-aggressive behavior I:

- Chose to hide my reaction because I did not want others to know I was uncomfortable
- Made decisions for others and myself
- Got what I wanted but it may have been at the other person's expense

I chose passive-aggressive behavior when I (list examples):

1.
2.
3.

I chose passive-aggressive behavior most during this week when I was dealing with people (circle one):

1. At work
2. In my family
3. Who are close friends
4. In social situations
5. Who were strangers
6. Other

I am dissatisfied with the way I dealt with _____

because_____

If I could do it differently, I might _____

Aggressive Behavior

If I chose aggressive behavior I:
- Got my own needs met regardless of the needs of others
- Took responsibility for making my own decisions and also for the decisions of others
- Was not concerned about hiding my reaction (may have made others uncomfortable)

I chose aggressive behavior when I (list examples):
1.
2.
3.

I chose aggressive behavior most during this week when I was dealing with people (circle one):
7. At work
8. In my family
9. Who are close friends
10. In social situations
11. Who were strangers
12. Other

I am dissatisfied with the way I dealt with _____
because_____
If I could do it differently, I might _____
_____

Assertive Behavior

If I chose assertive behavior I:
- Let others know what my needs were and asked others to recognize those needs
- Recognized the needs of others
- Negotiated a solution that was agreeable to all parties
- Took responsibility for meeting my own needs

I chose assertive behavior when I (list examples):
1.
2.
3.

I chose assertive behavior most during this week when I was dealing with people (circle one):
1. At work
2. In my family
3. Who are close friends
4. In social situations
5. Who were strangers
6. Other

I am dissatisfied with the way I dealt with _____
because_____
If I could do it differently, I might _____

_____

After doing these exercises ask yourself the following questions: Were you assertive as consistently as you thought? What is your default behavior? What pattern or tendency did you notice? Is it easier to be assertive with people you are close to or is it more difficult? Are you now better able to identify the behavior exerted by yourself and others?

The first step in chasing away the spirits of the staircase is being able to focus your awareness on how others behave and then identify what sort of behavior that elicits in you. In order to gain confidence, you must feel some control. In order to feel control, you must be able to identify and name the behavior that you observe in yourself and others. You must be able to take a step back as if you were an objective observer and watch the others in the room. Then you must know yourself well enough to be able to predict your "default" patterns of behavior and if necessary correct them and choose the behavior that is in your best interest.

Now that you have had an opportunity to increase your awareness and insight into the behavior of others, it is important that you focus on what you want for yourself. If you bought this book, chances are you want to be more effective in your personal and professional life. The next step is to set goals for yourself to make this a reality.

Goal Setting Exercise

List two personal or professional situations where you would like to be more effective.

1.

2.

Describe how you will approach each of the above situations.

1.

2.

Take home message: The more you practice, the quicker you get. The quicker you get, the more successful you will be. The more successful you are, the more confident you will become.

CHAPTER 5

The Magic Formula

CLAIRE SHIPMAN, A REPORTER FOR ABC News and Katty Kay, anchor for BBC World News in America are authors of the book, *The Confidence Code: The Science and Art of Self-Assurance – What Women Should Know.*[1] In the May 2014 edition of *The Atlantic,* the authors report, "The shortage of female confidence is increasingly well quantified and well documented. In 2011, the Institute of Leadership and Management, in the United Kingdom, surveyed British managers about how confident they feel in their professions. Half the female respondents reported self-doubt about their job performance and careers, compared with fewer than a third of male respondents." They went on to say that in study after study men overestimate their abilities and performance and women underestimate both. This occurs even when their performances did not differ in quality from their male colleagues. The authors found that women apply for promotions only when they meet 100% of job qualifications while men were likely to apply when they met only 50% of the required credentials. This lack of confidence can be devastating to women. Kay and Shipman are clear to point out that success correlates just as closely with confidence as it does with competence.

The implications are clear. If we as women aren't self-confident, we run the risk of losing out. How do we increase our self-confidence? I propose that we do so by being able to identify how others are behaving and choose a behavior that will increase the probability we will get what we want, but more importantly, increase the probability that our self-confidence will not suffer if we don't!

These authors have done an important part of the work for us. In addition to naming the problem, they point out that women must acquire the skills to take action. Confidence and taking action appear to be closely related. The authors state, "Confidence is a belief in one's ability to succeed, a belief that stimulates action. In turn, taking action bolsters one's belief in one's ability to succeed. So confidence accumulates— through hard work, through success, and even through failure."[1] What typically holds women back is not their actual ability but their choice not to try. Their advice to women to become more confident is to stop thinking so much and just act.

Almost daily, new evidence emerges of just how much our brains can change over the course of our lives. As we learn to shift to healthier thought patterns and effective behavioral techniques we have the potential to make our brains more confidence-prone. If you play a sport or musical instrument you know that there are fundamentals that you had to learn in order to play the game or perform musically. The same is true with behavior. I read this as a call to action for those of us who are trained to teach the methods of behavioral change. In this book we will learn the skills necessary to increase the probability that we will **try**, that we will **act**, and that we will take a step toward empowerment by increasing our confidence in our personal and professional interactions. In the next chapter we will look at some of the fundamental behavioral skills to accomplish these goals.

Take home message: Women's lack of self-confidence impedes their ability to try. Without effort there can be no success. This vicious cycle can be broken by adopting a skill set — let's call it the magic formula — to move us forward when we are stuck.

References

1. Kay, K. Shipman, C. (2014) **The Confidence Code: The Science and Art of Self-Assurance – What Women Should Know.** New York, NY: HarperCollins Publishers Inc.

CHAPTER 6

Armed and Dauntless

I AM GOING TO SAY SOMETHING to you in three different ways. I want you to get in touch with how you feel after each statement.

Statement 1: "You did not call me last night. What the hell? You never do what you say you're going to do. You always say you will call and then you don't."
Statement 2: "So, what did you do last night?"
Statement 3: "I was really disappointed when you did not call me at 7 PM as we had pre-arranged because I really look forward to our phone chats."

Chances are you felt defensive when you heard the first statement. Chances are you felt nothing at all when you heard the second statement. Perhaps you felt a tinge of remorse or regret when you heard the third statement. Which statement increases the probability that the next time we arrange for a telephone conference, you will actually follow through? Most of you would say the third statement. If you are the individual who was wronged, which way increases the probability that you will feel okay about the way you confronted the individual who did not follow through on the telephone call? Again, most of you would choose the last statement.

Let's explore. Imagine if I was supposed to call you and did not follow through. You confronted me, using the tone and vocabulary of the first statement, and I responded with something like, "I am so sorry, but my kitten ingested a ribbon and I had to take her to the emergency room. They had to perform an emergency endoscopy. I almost lost her, but thankfully she will be okay." You would likely feel terrible for having confronted me inappropriately. With the second statement, the individual who did not follow through on his/her commitment doesn't even know what you are talking about. If the telephone call completely slipped their mind, they might think that you are simply making an inquiry about what they did the night before. The third statement invites the other person to step into the assertive circle. It simply says I was disappointed that you didn't call because I look forward to our calls. Incidentally that's a very difficult statement to argue with. If I say I was disappointed you didn't call, a response of "no you weren't" doesn't even make sense.

I Feel When Because

Let's break down the statements above and look at each component. In the first statement we start with the word "you," which is accusatory and puts the other person on the defensive (an aggressive statement). The third statement is what we call an *I Feel When Because* statement (an assertive statement). In this type of statement we share our feelings... *I was disappointed.* Then we get specific and add **when** to clarify what elicited these feelings... *when you did not call me at 7 PM as pre-arranged.* The second statement does not describe feelings or give specifics — it's vague and unclear (a passive-aggressive statement). To finish an *I Feel When Because* statement we add a "hook"... *I really look forward to our phone chats.* This assures the other person that you are not intending to criticize them, you are simply acknowledging that contact with them is important to you. This formula of *I Feel When Because* can be extremely effective. It can be your "fallback" whenever you are stuck for something to say. It communicates to the other person that you are requesting engagement and participation on their part. It is an invitation to step into the assertive circle. Practice the *I Feel When Because* so that it becomes almost automatic when you are in a conflictual situation.

In the next exercise, you will have the opportunity to practice the *I Feel When Because* statements.

The "I" Message

The "I" message is a way of stating your position and your feelings while respecting the rights of others. The "I" message can be positive or negative.

The elements of the "I" message are:
1. State your feeling...
   I feel_____.
2. Describe the behavior that caused the feeling (be very specific)...
   When _____.
3. Explain the consequences for you (this is your hook)...
   Because_____.

Example: Your co-worker comes back from lunch a half hour late. You are upset because you will miss a half hour of your own break. You say:

I feel ... *annoyed*
When... *you return from lunch a half hour late.*
Because ... *I can't leave and I miss a half hour of my own lunch break.*

Practice the "I" message in the following situations:

1. Your co-worker fills in for you. When you return you say (Hint: this is a positive one):

2. Your supervisor criticizes you in front of co-workers and a subordinate. You see her privately later and say:

3. One employee interrupts you when you are talking to another employee. You say:

INCREASING YOUR PERSONAL AND PROFESSIONAL EFFECTIVENESS

A Manual for Women Who Want to Accomplish More Without Changing Who They Are

4. You are trying to concentrate and complete a project to meet a deadline. The person in your office who is known to be friendly, sociable, and sensitive, drops by your office to chat. You say:

5. Your boss tells you she is giving you a raise. You say:

6. Write your own dilemma here:

How did it go? Some folks have difficulty with the first scenario. You will find that *I Feel When Because* is a great way to compliment other people and build a sense of cohesion. If you notice we usually find it easier to be specific when we are complaining to someone about something. And yet, when we compliment someone we go to the general. For instance, you might say, "You look nice today" instead of "You look nice today and I especially like that color on you." Hopefully, by the time you got down to the last question you were able to write your own dilemma and formulate an *I Feel When Because* in a novel situation. If you have difficulty thinking of feeling words, I have included a list of them in the following diagram. Obviously some are more easily articulated than others, but it will give you an idea of where to start if it's difficult for you to get in touch with your feelings.

Feeling Words

Happy

Glad, ecstatic, elated, jubilant, exultant, joyful, pleased, eager

Contented

Pleased, satisfied, content

Sad

Disappointed, melancholy, sorry or sorrowful, discosolate, depressed, aggrieved

Excited

Energetic, eager, thrilled, anxious, restless, nervous, agitated, frantic, passionate, hysterical

Angry

Annoyed, irritated, distressed, aggravated, exasperated, indignant, offended, repelled, appalled, grouchy, mad, resentful, bitter, infuriated, enraged

Guilty

Regretful, remorseful, contrite, penitent

Envious

Jealous, greedy, grudging, possessive, suspicious

Affected

Hurt, touched, pleased, displeased, harassed, conrolled, ignored, unwanted, appreciated, unappreciated

Strong

Resolute, determined, powerful, definite, courageous

It is also ok to soften it a bit by saying something like... *I am confused as to why you didn't call when prearranged... or... It bewilders me when you... or... It is hard for me to understand why.*

Empathy Sandwich

Empathy Statement

Descriptive Statement

Specific Request

The assertive **Empathy Sandwich** may be your choice if you find you are not getting your needs met in a situation and you want to ask for something from another person. It shows your understanding of their position, describes your own, and asks for specific performance. Let's take a look at the following example. You are in a busy restaurant on your lunch hour and your order has not been taken. You call the waitress to your table, and you say:

Statement 1: "Hey! We've been sitting here for 10 minutes and we still don't have menus. What kind of place is this?"
Statement 2: You do not ask for the server or manager but instead grumble to your tablemate about the terrible service and refuse to leave a tip.
Statement 3: "Wow, I can see this place has you hopping today, but I have been waiting quite a few minutes for my menu and I need to get back to work soon. I was wondering if I could just go ahead and order."

Obviously, the first statement is aggressive. The second statement is passive-aggressive because instead of dealing directly with the person who is responsible, you do nothing except complain to a third party who is powerless to solve the problem. The **Empathy Sandwich** (assertive) contains a statement of empathy towards the other person: *I can see this place really has you hopping today.* This makes a very clear description about the difficulty you (and the server) are experiencing. You then use a descriptive statement to make your position clear: *I've been waiting quite a few minutes for my menu and I have to be back to work soon.* Then (and this is really important), you ask for a specific request: *I was wondering if I could just go ahead and order.* Any good salesman will tell you that you have to close the contract. They will say something like, "What do I have to do to get you into a new car today?" Do not fail to leave the request off the end of your *Empathy Sandwich*. On the following pages you are given situations in which you can practice delivering the *Empathy Sandwich*.

Making Requests: The Assertive Empathy Sandwich

As you create an empathy sandwich for the below situations, follow this structure: Show you understand the other party's position (empathy), describe your own, then ask for a specific performance.

Situations:

1. Your child has been watching Saturday morning cartoons and you want him to clean his room before you leave for a family picnic at noon. You say:

2. Your Administrative Assistant is having a long conversation with a co-worker and you need a task assigned to her to be completed quickly. You say:

3. You are responsible for conducting a staff meeting. You have stressed the importance of punctuality. One of your staff members arrives 45 minutes late for the meeting. He mumbles an apology and gives a vague reference to a crisis with a patient or customer. You say:

4. Your boss has just given you a new assignment. In order for the assignment to be completed successfully you must make sure that your staff participates actively. Your staff is already overwhelmed.

   a. What do you say to your boss?

   b. What do you say to your staff?

5. Your staff sense that dramatic changes are coming and you have recently been behind closed doors with top administration. During a staff meeting they ask you a question, the answer to which you cannot reveal. You say:

INCREASING YOUR PERSONAL AND
PROFESSIONAL EFFECTIVENESS

A Manual for Women Who Want to Accomplish
More Without Changing Who They Are

DESC Script

If the techniques we have discussed so far backfire and the person refuses to step into the assertive circle, it is time to elevate the interaction. This is where the **DESC Script** comes into play. The **DESC Script**, as offered by Sharon Anthony Bower,[1] is a way of confronting another person's negative behavior in situations that do not involve ongoing personal relationships. It's similar to the *I Feel When Because* message, but it goes several steps farther. In addition to describing another person's behavior and expressing your feelings about it, you also specify what the other person needs to do in order to hold them accountable. This technique is more confrontational than the *I Feel When Because* statement or the *Empathy Sandwich*. The following lists the components of the DESC script:

D – *Describe* the other person's behavior objectively to him/her
E – *Express* your feelings to the other person in a calm way
S – *Specify* one or two behavior changes you would like the person to make and ask for agreement
C – Tell the person what you will do for them if the agreement is honored (positive *Consequences*) and tell the person what you will do if they do not honor the agreement (negative *Consequences*)

Let me show you how this works with the following example. Your child throws a temper tantrum in the grocery store because you won't buy her a candy bar. First, you need to *describe* the other person's behavior objectively to him or her. You might say, "Katy, screaming and crying is not appropriate." Next, *express* your feelings to the other person in a calm way. You could state, "I am very disappointed that you have chosen to act this way." Follow with the *specific* behaviors you need the person to change and ask for agreement. You could say, "I know that you have the ability to use words and ask me politely for what you would like. Do you think you can do that right now?" Next, follow with the *consequences,* both positive and negative. This might look something like, "If you behave in a calm way and use your words, I am more likely to allow you to come with me the next time I go to the store. If you do not stop screaming and crying, not only will I not let you go to the store with me next time, but I will leave the store with you right now. We will sit in the car until you can behave the way you know you are supposed to." Now it is your turn to give this technique a try. On the following pages you are given situations in which you can practice delivering a **DESC script**.

Making Requests: The DESC Script

As you create a DESC Script for the below situations follow this structure: describe the behavior, express your feelings, specify the change required, and provide both the negative and positive consequences.

Situations:

1. You had agreed upon an estimate to have your car repaired with the auto shop. When you get the bill you are charged $200 more. You say:

2. You have had numerous conversations with an employee about complying with deadlines. Each time he promises to cooperate in meeting the required deadlines, but then he does not follow through. You say:

3. A staff member teases you in front of other staff and occasionally in front of your boss. You have asked him to stop a few times. Each time he laughs it off and says, "You are just too sensitive. I was just kidding. Where is your sense of humor?" You say:

4. You are giving feedback to an employee who doesn't want to hear it. She becomes angry, agitated, and aggressive. She raises her voice and begins pacing around your office. You say:

The *I Feel When Because*, the *Empathy Sandwich,* and the *DESC Script* are fundamental techniques that you should be able to use at will. Admittedly, you can move on the continuum from the assertive point towards the aggressive or to passive, but remember, some techniques are best used in situations where you do not have an ongoing relationship with the person, such as customer to a place of business, or you clearly have power over the person to whom you are speaking, such as parent and child. The *I Feel*

When Because statements extend the invitation to the other person to step into the assertive circle and negotiate with you. There are other techniques that lean toward a passive aggressive place on the continuum. Remember what we said in the beginning, there is no value judgment on using any of these behaviors. You simply need to choose one that fits the situation the best, or that is in your best interest. If you continuously request that the other person step into the assertive circle with you and they continue to be aggressive, then you can move on the continuum to match them. If you choose a different behavior, always return to the assertive circle at the first opportunity. Let's take a look at some other techniques.

Broken Record

Broken Record is simply giving yourself permission to stick to your guns. If someone is trying to manipulate you into doing something you don't want to do, you simply persist in saying no. You tell yourself that regardless of the reasons that the other person gives you, it is a task you don't want to do. They may be requesting something that offends your value system or you simply don't have time, but whatever the reason, you want to say no. So you simply continue to say no repeatedly. It might go something like this:

Other person: "I want you to take minutes at our next committee meeting."

You: "I really won't be able to do that."

Other person: "Why not?"

You: "I won't be able to do that."

Other person: "But you're so good at it. You've done this at all of our meetings and your minutes are always so accurate."

You: "Precisely, I feel as though I am the only one taking minutes. I would like someone else to take a turn."

Other person: "Oh, but no one is as good at it as you are."

You: "I appreciate your vote of confidence, however I will not be able to do it."

Other person: "Please?"

You: "Once again, I appreciate your flattery, but I won't be able to comply at this time."

Note in the preceding exchange you had to move to an *I Feel When Because* statement since the broken record was not enough. Notice too that you do not offer an excuse or compelling evidence. You simply say NO consistently and politely, but firmly.

Content Process Shift

Content Process Shift is determination on your part to not get sucked into the vortex of arguing with the other person over the issue at hand. Rather, you point out to the other person that they are being aggressive. It goes something like this:

Other person: "I want you to take minutes at the next meeting."

You: "I won't be able to do that."

Other person: "Why not?"

You: "I believe that I have taken minutes for the last three meetings and I would like someone else to take a turn." (*I Feel When Because* statement)

Other person: "But you're so good at it."

You: "I appreciate the vote of confidence, but I won't be able to comply at this time."

Other person: "What is it with you anyway? I mean, I can't believe you are giving me a hard time over this. How difficult would it be? You do it so easily."

You: Do not get sucked into the content explaining why it would be difficult for you. It would sound like this: "It's hard for me to listen and take notes at the same time." This statement will invite the other person to challenge your reasoning. Instead simply say, "You seem to be trying to manipulate me into doing something that I don't want to do. I'm not sure how much more clear I can be. I won't be taking minutes at the next meeting."

The key to this technique is rather than getting sucked into an argument about the content, you are focusing on the process that the other person is being unfair to you by trying to manipulate you.

Fogging
The final technique that will be useful to you is called **Fogging**. Fogging is a bit more passive aggressive in that you are purposely attempting to obfuscate. In other words, no matter how passive aggressive or aggressive the other person gets, you simply deflect or good naturedly refuse. It might look something like this:

Other person: "I want you to take notes at the next meeting."

You: "Do these hands look bionic to you?" (Smiling the whole time.) "I've taken notes so many times I'm beginning to get writer's cramp. How about giving someone else a turn?"

Other person: "But you're so good at it."

You: "Flattery will get you nowhere my friend. I've already decided that this is not the meeting for me to be taking notes. Maybe next time."
Fogging is simply standing your ground and being good-natured about it. It can even be playful in cases such as this:
Other person introduces a friend who is a government employee: "This is my friend who works for the government — you know what that means. This is my friend who does not work at all."

Friend: "Yup, that's me, just eating at the trough on the taxpayers' expense. That's how I can afford my luxury cars and my mega mansion."

In other words, instead of taking offense, acting insulted, or sulking, you imply that the insult is so absurd that it is laughable. By playing along good naturedly, this inoculates you against future insults because it fails to pique your ire. This technique is frequently observed between men who will goad one another when they feel comradery. This concept is foreign to women.

By virtue of the communication patterns established in western culture, some of these techniques are easier for men, and others are easier for women. For example, in our culture we typically do not hear men talking about their feelings as frequently as women do. Can you imagine a man saying, "I feel hurt when you criticize me in front of the other men." On the other hand, it would be perfectly acceptable to hear a man say something like, "Hey buddy, what the hell? You put me down in front of the team." He is likely to be laughing and being good-natured about it. Another illustration would look like this. Two couples meet each other on the street – they haven't seen one another in years. The women embrace and say, "Oh my God, you look fabulous. How long has it been since we've seen each other?" Can you imagine the men doing this? Of course not. But the men might say something like, "Hey pal, you're looking good." Whereupon the man who has just been complimented might pat his stomach and say, "Well a few too many *brewskies*, but all in all, I'm doing okay." Can you imagine a woman patting her abdomen and saying that she "had a few too many Brewskies?" Well, you get the idea.

Bared Throat

Fogging is very kin to bared throat. **Bared throat** is used when you genuinely have made a mistake. Instead of trying to hide the mistake or becoming defensive because you have made a mistake, you admit to the mistake and apologize pre-emptively. Let's say for example that it was your responsibility to prepare the agenda for a meeting and you forgot to do so. The meeting is about to start and your boss is very displeased that an agenda has not been distributed. Before this displeasure erupts into public criticism, you simply say, "I am so terribly sorry, but I was unable to complete the agenda prior to this meeting." You do not offer an excuse that can be argued. That's what kids do when they've forgotten their homework and you don't want the other person to assume the role of the teacher. Instead, apologize and offer a solution such as, "I am so terribly sorry, I have made an error. I apologize for the inconvenience. Allow me to remedy the situation by generating an agenda on the white board right now." That kind of takes the wind out of the sails of anyone who would criticize you because then they come across as a bully. After all, once you apologize and offer a remedy, they can either join in and help you with the remedy, or they can express their dismay. If the latter occurs, you accept it because it was your error, apologize again, and move on. If they berate you, they are going to come across as the bully and the group will more than likely side with you. After all, everyone makes mistakes.

Let's review what you have learned so far. You should be able to identify behavior along the continuum. In other words, you can identify when someone is being passive-aggressive, passive, aggressive, and assertive. You have also practiced using your *I Feel When Because*, *Empathy Sandwiches* and your **DESC Scripts**. Depending on the situation and the relationship you have with the other party, choose which communication technique is best for the situation. This will allow you to invite the other party into the assertive circle. Perhaps most important of all is to practice, practice, practice. Just like the musician practices before a performance or an athlete rehearses fundamentals to be ready to use in a game, you must become fluent in these behaviors. I refer back to the book, *The Confidence Code*, where the authors were clear to point out that success correlates just as closely with confidence as it does with competence. Confidence and taking action appear to be closely related.

You now have the skills so start building your confidence by practicing these skills and remember, not only do you gain value from successes, but you also gain from failures. If you are a typically passive person, choose a low risk situation and become aggressive just to see what it feels like. Likewise, if you are seen as an aggressive person, hold-back during a low risk situation to see how it feels and note how others regard you. If you do this often enough, you will become more facile in choosing which behavior is appropriate. This puts you in control instead of going to a default behavior, which is predictable and not as effective.

We are now ready to move on to Part II of this book. This section contains the real life scenarios presented by women who participated in my seminars with commentary and analysis so that you can see how the behaviors that were chosen produced the desired effect

Take home message: Remember there is no right or wrong when choosing a technique. You may move up or down the behavioral continuum and then return to the assertive circle. When you want to invite someone into the assertive circle choose from a variety of techniques that are listed in this chapter. Practice each technique in low risk situations until they become so automatic that you can use them at will.

References:

1. Bower, S. Potter, B. (1976) **Asserting Yourself: A Practical Guide for Positive Change.** Addison-Wesley Reading, MA: Publishing Company.

PART TWO
THE STORIES

CHAPTER 7

Dealing with the Aggressive Boss: Angela's Story

Each participant in the seminar submitted a sample of a conflictual situation that happened to her outside of the seminar. Most of the participants prefer to remain anonymous, so names and other identifiers have been changed to respect their wishes. The following is the scenario presented by Angela (not her real name).

Angela has always approached any interactions with colleagues with an open mind and a positive, nonjudgmental attitude. She would often feel discouraged when conversations had a negative tone or ended with an inconclusive decision. Was she approaching these encounters in an effective way? When presented with a confrontation or an uncomfortable situation, the default mode Angela was accustomed to was to evade, escape, and retreat back to a world of no confrontation.

Angela informed the group of a difficult situation that she encountered during a professional business meeting. She had recently started her new job and was approached to deliver an informational session about a new service her company was developing. Her boss informed her that he would be traveling during the previously scheduled presentation and asked Angela to represent the company on his behalf. Angela knew the only way to get others to buy-in to the idea was to think carefully about how her message would be crafted and delivered since the service was new and innovative. She knew there would be questions about why the new service was needed, beneficial, and effective. After hours of preparation and running through various scenarios in her mind, she felt prepared.

The day of her presentation she walked into the meeting with a sense of pride and confidence. She was representing her new company and new service. In fact, she knew she would be delivering the new service as part of her new role, so she felt extremely vested in ensuring its success. With little hesitation, Angela delivered a brief presentation regarding what her company was proposing and why the service was important. She felt energized, invigorated, and positive. When she finished talking, she looked briefly around the room with relief that no one looked confused, concerned, or upset about what she had explained. One individual asked a question regarding how this service would differ from the customary services. It was an easy question for Angela since she had explained new and innovative services within her field to both internal and external stakeholders before. She felt successful until the second question, or rather, comment, arose.

Barb, the chief operating officer (COO) of her own corporation, put her hand in the air. Angela felt her nerves on edge since Barb held such a lofty position in the company and reported directly to Angela's boss. She commented that Angela's proposal was a good one, however asked the audience to consider the implications of the proposed services on their existing services. Did individuals have all the information they needed to know about the new service? Was Angela explaining all the options correctly? Looking around, Angela quickly realized that the room's feeling turned from acceptance to skepticism. Barb proceeded to look around at individuals in the room and whispered quietly to her neighbor after she finished commenting. Angela realized that this dialogue may have just undermined her work, passion, and positive outlook on how she expected this day to unfold.

Barb pulled Angela aside after the meeting. She let Angela know that she just wanted to reinforce that the service being proposed was not well communicated across the company. It wasn't Angela's fault, per se, but Barb felt it was important that the company employees be well informed. Angela couldn't hear much of what Barb was saying, she simply was lost in trying to navigate her thoughts of how to move forward.

Knowing that her boss would want to know what had just unfolded, Angela notified her boss about the presentation and conflicting events.

Chapter 7: Dealing with the Aggressive Boss: Angela's Story

Apparently this was not the first time that Barb had commented on new proposals after she personally approved of the process.

Angela was distraught. She knew the Women's Leadership Group would have advice. Several women in the group suggested taking the passive role in the situation given the aggressive nature that Barb tended to display. They were concerned that aggressive actions would only exacerbate the situation. Angela felt better knowing that the group supported her decisions to be passive in this situation.

Feeling at ease, Angela went on with her week. On Friday, she attended a meeting outside of her workplace for the day and was checking her email casually while waiting for the meeting to begin.

FROM: Barb
TO: Angela
SUBJECT: Need to talk

Please call me.
Barb
Sent from my iPhone

Angela knew this couldn't be good. She immediately felt her face flush. Her heart raced. She didn't want to respond to this email or call Barb back. She called Jen, a mentor and colleague in the Women's Leadership Group to seek advice. Jen advised her to be passive, again, in this situation and to be extremely cordial as a way to offset Barb's potential aggression. Jen suggested calling Barb and just listening to what she had to say. Hearing Barb out was often the solution to many conflicts. Angela thanked Jen and mentally prepared for her phone call. She thought of Jen's advice as she dialed the phone.

It was immediately evident that Barb had read the email Angela had sent to her boss. Barb voiced that she felt Angela was miscommunicating her message to the company. Barb noted that she was supportive of Angela's efforts and always had been. Angela thanked Barb for her support and in the back of her mind was thinking … *Passive. Passive. Passive. Less words. Passive. Be grateful.* As an extrovert, Angela constantly struggled with the fact that sometimes silence was good. But in these types of situations, she was thankful for the silence and her advice from her mentors. She

69

hung up the phone feeling empowered, enlightened, and at peace-short term. But had she officially communicated to Barb that she did not like being embarrassed publicly and that there was a more acceptable way to communicate her concern? Or did she inadvertently reinforce Barb's undesirable behavior?

Now let's go back and analyze this scenario paragraph by paragraph.
Angela has always approached any interactions with colleagues with an open mind and a positive, nonjudgmental attitude. She would often feel discouraged when conversations had a negative tone or ended with an inconclusive decision. Was she approaching these encounters in an effective way? When presented with a confrontation or an uncomfortable situation, the default mode Angela was accustomed to was to evade, escape, and retreat back to a world of no confrontation.

Analysis: Angela is most comfortable when she moves towards the passive end of the continuum. She works harder to avoid a conflict than she does to face one.
Angela informed the group of a difficult situation that she encountered during a professional business meeting. She had recently started her new job and was approached to deliver an informational session about a new service her company was developing. Her boss informed her that he would be traveling during the previously scheduled presentation, and asked Angela to represent the company on his behalf. Angela knew the only way to get others to buy-in to the idea was to think carefully about how her message would be crafted and delivered since the service was new and innovative. She knew there would be questions about why the new service was needed, beneficial, and effective. After hours of preparation and running through various scenarios in her mind, she felt prepared.

Analysis: Angela was strategic in preparing various scenarios. It is important to prepare and to practice. At the same time it is important to keep in mind that this is not memorizing potential responses, but rather conceptualizing what you want from the interaction and how far you are willing to move on the continuum from assertive to aggressive or assertive to passive. Remember our primary goal is to feel satisfied about the way you handled this situation.

The day of her presentation she walked into the meeting with a sense of pride and confidence. She was representing her new company and new service. In fact, she knew she would be delivering the new service as part of her new role, so she felt extremely vested in ensuring its success. With little hesitation, Angela delivered a brief presentation regarding what her company was proposing and why the service was important. She felt energized, invigorated, and positive. When she finished talking, she looked briefly around the room with relief that no one looked confused, concerned, or upset about what she had explained. One individual asked a question regarding how this service would differ from the customary services. It was an easy question for Angela since she had explained new and innovative services within her field to both internal and external stakeholders before. She felt successful. Until the second question, or rather, comment, arose. Barb, the chief operating officer (COO) of the corporation, put her hand in the air. Angela felt her nerves on edge since Barb held such a lofty position in the company and reported directly to Angela's boss. She commented that Angela's proposal was a good one, however asked the audience to consider the implications of the proposed services on their existing services. Did individuals have all the information they needed to know about the new service? Was Angela explaining all the options correctly? Looking around, Angela quickly realized that the room's feeling turned from acceptance to skepticism. Barb proceeded to look around at individuals in the room and whispered quietly to her neighbor after she finished commenting. Angela realized that this dialogue may have just undermined her work, passion, and positive outlook on how she expected this day to unfold.

Analysis: At this point Angela has a decision to make. Does she confront Barb publicly or does she ignore Barb's comment hoping that it doesn't gain traction? As you read above, Angela chooses passive behavior and ends up feeling okay about that. Had I had the opportunity to coach Angela at the time I probably would have suggested that she move from her comfort zone of ignoring the comment and move towards assertiveness. This is why. Angela allowed Barb to be aggressive and then as we shall see in the next paragraph, passive aggressive. Over time Barbara will be in a position to bully Angela. If Angela predictably becomes passive then Barbara becomes passive aggressive. Angela could have tried the *I Feel When Because* statement. It would sound

something like this: "Barbara, I am surprised that you are challenging the implications of the service I am proposing because I have very carefully taken the following into account (reiterate the point you wish to make about the advantage of the new product). Anyone in the room that is worried about this proposal is invited to meet with me privately because I feel confident I can address their concerns." Angela should immediately call on another participant and not give Barb an opportunity to challenge that statement. By using the *I Feel When Because* statement, Angela defends her position in a way that is difficult to refute. At the same time, if delivered in a professional tone it cannot be perceived as aggressive. The benefit to doing this is that she sends Barb the message that it is not acceptable to undermine her presentation. The risk is that Barb has more power than Angela and once thwarted may attempt to sabotage Angela in another way. It is this risk that more than likely prompted Angela to choose the passive route and feel okay about it.

Barb pulled Angela aside after the meeting. She let Angela know that she just wanted to reinforce that the service being proposed was not well communicated across the company. It wasn't Angela's fault, per se, but Barb felt it was important that the company employees be well informed. Angela couldn't hear much of what Barb was saying, she simply was lost in trying to navigate her thoughts of how to move forward.

Analysis: Barb is patronizing Angela, she is basically saying I know I sabotaged your presentation, but it really is in your best interest. Angela could have responded to Barb with an *Empathy Sandwich*. It would sound something like this: "Barb, I appreciate your attempt to protect the other employees by making sure they are well informed, but it would have been more helpful to me had you given me an opportunity to privately address those concerns. Next time, I would appreciate it if you would ask a question so that I have an opportunity to clarify rather than challenge me publicly. Do you think that is something you would be comfortable doing given the power differential in our roles?" By describing Barbara's behavior with clarity and making a request, Angela communicates to Barb that she is savvy and clearly understands what is going on. She is also asking Barb if her veiled attempt at assuaging her negative feelings is Barb's way of pointing out that Angela is to follow

Barb's directives. In which case, Barb should have made that clear prior to this presentation.

Knowing that her boss would want to know about what had just unfolded, Angela notified her boss. Apparently this was not the first time that Barb had commented on new proposals after she personally approved of the process.

Analysis: Angela is seeking solace from someone who outranks Barb. It is not unusual for women to seek validation when they are feeling uncomfortable. Seeking support can sometimes be helpful, but it should be done with the risks in mind. In this case Angela's superior was not at all invested in Angela's feelings and simply emailed a copy of Angela's communication to Barb. Had Angela confronted Barb individually, she would have effectively communicated that she would not allow herself to be bullied or patronized. By keeping it between the two of them she neutralizes Barb's attempt. By involving Barb's boss, Barb is now invested in being "right" because she has to defend her position.

Angela was distraught. She knew the Women's Leadership Group would have advice. Several women in the group suggested taking the passive role in the situation given the aggressive nature that Barb tended to display. Aggressive actions would only exacerbate the situation. Angela felt better knowing that the group supported her decisions to be passive in this situation.

Feeling at ease, Angela went on with her week. On Friday, she attended a meeting outside of her workplace for the day, and was checking her email casually while waiting for the meeting to begin.

FROM: Barb
TO: Angela
SUBJECT: Need to talk

Please call me.
Barb
Sent from my iPhone

Angela knew this couldn't be good. She immediately felt her face flush, her heart raced. She didn't want to respond to this email or call Barb back. She called Jen, a mentor and colleague in the Women's Leadership Group to seek advice. Jen advised her to be passive, again, in this situation and to be extremely cordial as a way to offset Barb's potential aggression. Jen suggested calling Barb and just listening to what she had to say. Hearing Barb out was often the solution to many conflicts. Angela thanked Jen and mentally prepared for her phone call. She thought of Jen's advice as she dialed the phone.

Analysis: This is an example of how retreating to your comfort level gives you a false sense of security. Having said that, it is understandable that the group who interfaces with Barb frequently would caution Angela about confronting Barb. Clearly, if you are going to be assertive you must be prepared to take the risks. Not everyone appreciates assertiveness, particularly not individuals that are aggressive or passive aggressive and are used to getting their own way. When you become assertive you inevitably communicate that you are not going to be a victim of aggression or passive aggression. So the other person is not always going to get their way and this can be threatening. Once again, you have to ask yourself which behavior will ultimately contribute to your confidence and your sense of empowerment. This phone conversation is an example of a false sense of security. Being passive can make the pain go away short term, but it leaves the door open for someone who is very comfortable being passive or passive aggressive. At the same time, Jen's advice cautioning Angela not be aggressive is good advice, but there is another alternative available and that alternative is being assertive.

It was immediately evident that Barb had read the email Angela had sent to her boss. Barb voiced that she felt Angela was miscommunicating her message to the company. Barb noted that she was supportive of Angela's efforts, and always had been. Angela thanked Barb for her support and in the back of her mind was thinking *Passive. Passive. Passive. Less words. Passive. Be grateful.* As an extrovert, Angela constantly struggled with the fact that sometimes silence was good. But in these types of situations, she was thankful for the silence and her advice from her mentors. She hung up the phone feeling empowered, enlightened, and at peace.

Analysis: Angela verifies that she believes the message that Barb is being supportive. However, Barb's message should be interpreted with caution. While Angela may feel empowered, enlightened, and at peace "short term", Barb cannot be trusted. Anyone that is aggressive in public and passive aggressive afterwards is comfortable using those tactics. While Angela can feel good about not arguing with Barb, which would not have been in her best interest, she could have once again used an *I Feel When Because* statement. She could say, "I am so pleased that you are supportive of my project, however I am confused about the way you express your support. When you challenged me publicly during my presentation it sounded as though you were asking the other people in the room to turn down my proposal. Now you are telling me that you are supportive of my proposal? Perhaps we need to discuss which portions of my proposal you can endorse without reservation, and which parts cause you concern. Shall we set up a time to do that?"

In considering this scenario, Angela demonstrates behaving in a passive way and that apparently feels okay for her. If, however, Barb continues to behave in a way that causes Angela to be haunted by the spirits of the staircase, then Angela needs to learn to be more assertive when dealing with Barb. It is to Angela's credit at no time did she become aggressive with Barb. It would have been very easy to put Barb on the defensive by saying something such as, "Why did you tell other people in the room to be suspicious of my proposal? You were clearly sabotaging my program." (aggressive statement). That almost certainly leads to a prolonged conversation where Barb has to defend her position or pull rank and simply tell Angela it is not going to be discussed. By using *I Feel When Because* statements and *Empathy Sandwiches*, Angela can effectively communicate to Barb that she had better think twice about being aggressive or passive aggressive. This lets Barb know that Angela is able to handle both in a way that invites Barb to step into the assertive circle and genuinely have a mutually respectful discussion about Angela's proposal as it relates to Barb's position. Arguably that would facilitate Angela's feeling empowered not just short term, but in future dealings with Barb.

Take home message: Sometimes you have to teach people how to treat you. Don't choose to be passive by denying there is a problem or avoiding conflict and then justifying it by announcing to yourself that you feel better because you were nice to the person who just took advantage of you. If you do you are encouraging them to continue to manipulate you and you run the risk of losing their respect and ultimately your own self-respect.

CHAPTER 8

Avoiding the Flame Thrower: Jennifer's Story

WHEN YOU REACH AN INTERMEDIATE step in your career ladder, the rules for professional communication and courtesy seem to become less definite. In the world of communicating by email, the lines of professionalism can become even more blurred. As a fourth year pharmacy student finishing my final clinical year before becoming licensed, I witnessed this lack of professionalism first hand. I begin my story by painting the setting for an interaction I had with a first year pharmacy student.

I have an interest in academia and was fortunate enough to have a rotation at a school of pharmacy, helping to teach students. From day one, I knew that I wanted to make an impact on the first year students, teaching them about professionalism and how they should plan for success over the next three years. I approached this teaching experience as I have many other times in the past, knowing that I wanted to be approachable yet command my audience. The pharmacist that I was working under allowed for this type of interaction by empowering me to become an extension of herself in the academic setting. One of the objectives was being responsible for grading the work of students in her class.

The particular essay I was grading was meant to be written as if they were a pharmacist or patient and reflect upon specific interactions of a patient and pharmacist. The goal was to implore students to think about the importance of that relationship and reflect on what it means for patient care. While there were many great essays, some individuals missed the mark on the objective of the essay. As a result, these students were allowed to re-write it and not be penalized if they resubmitted. I sent multiple emails to students offering feedback as a compliment sandwich; I complemented the strengths of their writing, explained what they needed to do differently and then asked them to please resubmit the piece. Also, I was very clear that I was grading their essays acting on behalf of the current teacher. They had interacted with me in orientation and most knew my role. All but one apologized for not reading the assignment carefully enough and sent their resubmissions.

One student chose a different path that proved to be very stressful for me. As I sat reading his original essay, it was remarkable to me how much thought he had put into his career choice and what it meant to be a pharmacist. The entire essay was written beautifully, although it did not fit the objectives for the essay. I wrote him an email as I did the others.

Hi Mitchell,

I'm helping Dr. Smith grade reflection essays and I was really pleased with the level of your writing! However, the assignment was to write from the first person perspective of the pharmacist or patient. Please revise your original submission and send your reflection to me by email by no later than Friday morning at 8:00 a.m. Please let me know if you have any questions.

*Thanks,
Jennifer*

I was expecting the same response that I received from the other students when I opened my email and read:

I'm sorry. I don't understand. I wrote in the FIRST person.

Please note the format of the email. My instincts were on high alert. There was a lack of formality as if he was writing a text message by not including the email sender or receiver. Not to mention the capitalization of the word first as if he were overemphasizing or yelling. His response irritated me from the first word. Not because of his directness, but because of his lack of professionalism in his communication and lack of formality. I was taught growing up that as you learn more about a person, only then can you develop a less formal tone in your interactions with them. This first year student could not even be bothered with the courtesy of addressing me and I certainly did not give him any clues that he could de-escalate his level of formality with me. But maybe I was being too harsh. I responded less kindly than before due to my irritation and hoped that this was just one isolated incident because he was in a hurry. I also included a PDF document on professional communication.

Hi Mitchell,

The assignment was to write from the first person as if you were the pharmacist (Dr. Lewis) or the patient (Elsa) not as first person as a pharmacy student.

Jennifer

I received back....

Dear Jennifer,

Ok, how much is this assignment worth? I'm really bogged down with reading this week.

My first response was utter disbelief in the amount of disrespect he was showing for his professor and myself, which I was amazed by this early on in his career. If I had received this email as a first year student, I would have apologized, looked at the instructions to find out where I went wrong, and then resubmitted with no questions asked. I was familiar with the curriculum and in the first week of classes so there is little going on that would require a student to feel "bogged down". Secondly, I would expect this response from a close friend and not a student to whom I was assigning a grade. Most students have a sense of respect for upperclassmen. There exists a basic level of respect in all professional interactions that is expected of professors and students of our institution. While everyone interprets professionalism and respect differently, fundamental rules should still be known and followed. I explained this to him in an email, as well as my continued desire for a rewritten essay. I expected him to respond with a greater sense of understanding and a new version of his essay. Instead his response was…

Dear Jennifer,

I'm sorry if you thought I was disrespectful, that was not at all my intention. I realized I was talking to a fellow student, not a professor, so I thought a bit of informality would be acceptable. I apologize if you did not see it that way.

I added some minor changes to my essay, but I need you to understand that I am very proud of the essay I submitted. I am passionate about what I do and my words reflect that, after all this was a reflection, not fiction.

I will accept whatever grade you're willing to give me for this.

Mitchell Brown

The professor that assigned this topic had very specific intentions as to what they wanted the students to learn from this assignment and it was not in his power to decide a different topic was more appropriate. The essay was not changed aside from a few words. I was once again angry that this student thought this was acceptable behavior for someone of his status. As he progresses through the curriculum, there will be many things that he disagrees with, but questioning the professor and blatantly disregarding instructions is not acceptable for someone in a learning position. Furthermore, there should be a level of courtesy expressed to all students and faculty regardless of their position. This is what I had hoped to express to him in the next email.

Hi Mitchell,

Yes, your tone did come off as disrespectful. As an upperclassman, I by no means see myself as the caliber of any of the faculty. However, there still is a minimal level of respect that we deserve as someone who has passed through the coursework and is helping to lead your classes. I do not mind some informality but that can be judged by someone's first email to you. The formality with which they address you should be mirrored by you in return, until you have reason to see it otherwise. I very clearly associated myself with Dr. Smith and my role as grader of your work. If the roles were reversed, I would take that as I should come off as cordial as possible with my return email and do what was being asked of me.

You wrote a fantastic essay, and if you recall, that was the first thing I told you in my original email. I was very impressed by your insights and the level of your writing at this stage in your career. However, your lack of willingness to want to better your essay also shows disrespect for what your professors are trying to teach you. They had a specific goal in mind for this essay and what they wanted you to get out of it. It was not your job to think you had something better to say and re-write your own format, no matter how good it was.

I am only trying to help you. There is much that you can learn from every opportunity that you are given at this institution. To fully reap the benefits you must also be humble enough to realize when you need to make changes. We are all here to learn.

I will discuss with Dr. Smith how she wishes to proceed with your grade.

Jennifer

This should have been the end of the conversation but he could not accept responsibility for his shortcoming and continued on.

Dear Jennifer,

I am still very confused at what I did wrong. I don't understand how something as personal as a reflection could be wrong. It's almost like an opinion, and I don't view anyone's opinion as wrong. I read a fellow classmate's essay to see if I was missing something in the instructions, but I couldn't really find anything wrong. She expressed her reflection, but did not get an email to rewrite it.

If you can tell me specifically what I did not do to complete the objectives in the overview, I will be glad to change them. But nowhere does it say it has to be written as fiction, only that it has to be written as a reflection. I thank you for enjoying my essay, but please understand that I was passionate and proud of that essay. And the fact that it's opinion-based makes it difficult for me to accept that my reflection and opinion is wrong.

Sincerely,
Mitchell Brown

If I could go back, I would have stopped responding at this point because there was no new information that I could offer and my position was not changing. Something that I have learned about myself is that I do not like to finish arguments without everyone on the same page and some agreement being reached. I am very uncomfortable with agreeing to disagree, especially when I am in a position above someone else and my decision is what matters. I don't ever want to leave a conversation with someone being unhappy with me. I tried to end this conversation on a positive note and help him further understand what he did wrong.

Mitchell,

Your opinion was not wrong, in fact it was very well expressed. However, you missed the point of the exercise. It was not meant to be fiction just to be written from within either the patient or the pharmacists head based on the answers you received to questions that day.

This exercise is designed to have you write imaginatively, in the voice of another person, to describe that person's experiences. It is meant for you to imagine, and attempt to capture in writing, the "interior monologue" of the other person, imagining his or her thoughts and experiences from his or her perspective, rather than your own.

I will hand your grading over to Dr. Smith and she will decide how to handle it unless you wish to submit something different.

Jennifer

This final email, or so I thought, was not the end. He continued telling me that he could not find the instructions on the website and offered more excuses. I continued to tell him that he could still submit an essay but he chose not to. In the end, I did not respond to his final email where he offered to take a zero for the assignment. I felt as if he were trying to play into my sympathies also by signing the email with deepest apologies.

He ended up getting a zero for the assignment, which did not impact his final grade and he passed the course. I hoped that this experience had taught him somewhat of a lesson, although I knew that I would probably never be sure of that. However, the next week I was instructed to lead another group that included him. I did not want to switch groups because I knew it would be important to not shy away from the interaction, showing that I was acting as professionally toward him as possible and leading by example. After the session, he came up to me and apologized. I thanked him for approaching me but would not validate him with my normal response that the situation was "ok". He ended up crying and I could tell that this had truly affected him. My normal response again would be to feel badly for him in that moment, but I know that I did everything the proper way and this was validated by the professor as well.

Analysis:
This case study illustrates the dangers of e-mail. If you notice, the student was perfectly willing to antagonize the graduate student instructor as long as he had the protective veil of using e-mail. There is something reinforcing about sitting at your desk, perhaps in your pajamas surrounded by your favorite things, maybe even people who support you, and typing away with vigor. It is quite another thing to look someone in the eye and respond to their non-verbal communication. It has been well documented that 80% of communication is tone, volume, and non-verbal body language; only 20% is actual content of what is being said. As long as he could "argue" his position, he was more than happy to do so. As a bright student, known

for his analytical skills, he was quite prepared to defend his intellectual position. The only problem was the process, not the content.

When two (or more) people engage in arguing via e-mail, it is described as "flame throwing" in modern slang. Because the underlying tenant in this exchange is jockeying for a position of power between a graduate student instructor and an undergraduate student, the process versus the content becomes the focus of the problem.

The graduate student, Jennifer, perhaps unwittingly undermined her position of power by conducting an exchange via e-mail. The moment that Mitchell began to show disrespect and argue is the moment he should have been summoned to appear in person. Having said this, it is important to point out that Jennifer did a wonderful job of asking him to step into the assertive circle. Several times she explained what was being requested of him and worded it carefully to emphasize the positive *(Broken Record)*. When he responded belligerently, she needed to move up the continuum from assertive more towards aggression in order to ground herself in her position of power. To step it up, she could have used a *Content Process Shift*. Recall the key to this technique is rather than getting sucked into an argument about the content, you are focusing on the process that the other person is being unfair to you by trying to manipulate you.

Let's see how this would have played out if Jennifer had chosen to go with this technique.

Dear Mitchell,

Your last e-mail suggests that you are taking a position of opposition to my suggestions as to how you might adequately address the rubric required for this assignment. Please plan to meet me on (suggested date and time). If this is not convenient for you, please suggest alternative dates and times. If I do not hear from you by (insert date and time), I will assume that you are in agreement with the grade assigned. Please understand that you did not complete the assignment satisfactorily.

Thank you,
Jennifer

Note how Jennifer focused on the process... *You are taking a position of opposition to my suggestions as to how you might adequately address the rubric required for this assignment* **(Content Process Shift).** The reason for this intervention is because once someone becomes belligerent, oppositional, or defiant it is important for you to control the environment. He should not be permitted to throw flames from the comfort of his chosen environment. Indeed, the first opportunity that occurred when the two of them were face to face prompted him to be much more honest with his emotions. This points out once again, it is much easier to express hostility, anger, belligerence, defiance, opposition, and even recalcitrance from a distance than it is to negotiate with them in person. If he refuses to meet face to face, then he has been warned that he will be gambling with his grade. Notice she is not able to say he would fail, because her professor may not agree with failing him.

This leads to the second point of this analysis. The student is pointing out to the graduate student that her power base is wobbly, and he does not perceive her as someone who has the ability to assign him a grade or enforce a rubric. This is a very tenuous position and fortunately the graduate student was sufficiently "deputized" by the professor. However, had she stated, "I'm going to give you an 'F'" and the professor did not back her up in assigning him a failing grade she would have lost all authority to instruct not only this student but others.

If Mitchell is true to form, he will not accept the date and time she has offered. She has inoculated herself against this power play by inviting him to propose a different date and time. When they meet in person, Jennifer should begin with *I Feel When Because* statements and *Empathy Sandwiches* such as, "I'm happy you could take time out of your busy schedule to meet with me today. I know that as busy as we both are, this meeting is one more appointment we have to keep. However, I felt that it was important for me to carve out some time to assist you in salvaging what could potentially be a failing grade *(I Feel When Because Statement).* It is not my intention to argue with you, attempt to persuade you, or otherwise request that you change your essay if you are not motivated to do so. However, it is my job to inform you that if you do not address the rubric of this assignment no matter how brilliantly executed it is, you are in jeopardy of receiving a failing grade *(Empathy Sandwich)."* When he retorts with, "But let me give you all the reasons why this is a brilliant essay," or "I'm confused," Jennifer simply needs to state, "I will say this one more time and then I do not believe it will be necessary to say anything else. The assignment as you have currently written does not meet the rubric and you are in danger of receiving a failing grade. I believe I have gone above and beyond, in terms of taking time out to meet with you and instructing you as to how the assignment could be corrected. If you choose not to do so, then I can rest easy that I have done my job. Thank you, Mitchell, for taking time to meet with me **(DESC Script)**.*"* The conversation is then closed. Do not engage in any more argument, exchange, or explanation and if necessary politely leave the room observing business etiquette by saying, "I am afraid I have to leave now to get to my next appointment." Your goal is to establish your position of authority, not to persuade or reconcile with the student. Now obviously, the graduate student instructor (Jennifer) should have cleared this with the professor ahead of time so the professor would back her up with her assertion.

The intervention I have suggested is not "better" than what Jennifer actually did. Serendipitously, Mitchell was assigned to Jennifer's small group so he knew that he had better do something quick to get back into her good graces. Whether or not the tears were genuine or they were manipulative is irrelevant. He finally got the message that Jennifer was in a position of power over him. Whether that message was understood when he actually did receive the failing grade or whether or not that message would have been received had he been summoned to meet with her personally can never be known. Chances are, Jennifer would not be haunted by the spirits of the staircase.

Take home message: Do not engage in flame throwing. The longer a written exchange goes on, the more fodder there is for unresolved arguments.

CHAPTER 9

Spotting the Manipulator: Marie's Story

IN THIS CHAPTER WE CONTINUE our discussion of choosing to move on the behavioral continuum. This time we will focus on staying in the assertive circle. Let's take a look at Marie.

Marie has been a faculty member for 10 years and has participated in a number of communication activities but never really appreciated looking at the passive – assertive – aggressive spectrum. After learning about the spectrum, Marie was impressed to see how people respond in conversations and moved around the spectrum. She had an opportunity to practice with other senior faculty and university administration. Marie motivated herself to be assertive in a meeting where formerly she would have traditionally taken a more passive approach. The objective of the meeting was to allow everyone the opportunity to express his or her opinion and remark objectively in order to further a cause. The group would then achieve consensus considering all viewpoints. After initial greetings, discussion turned to a question about the new university facilities. Marie chimed in that the facilities were great but had observed that few people were using the center. This garnered a quick response from a more senior individual stating how there in fact was a significant amount of utilization, directly contradicting Marie. The next question was answered by Marie and then "corrected" with a different observation once again implying her observations were incorrect. Marie, having seen the swing on the spectrum to a passive-aggressive approach from the leader, opted to use a passive approach since there seemed to be "talking points" that were in direct contrast to her observations as noted by the senior official. Once she took this approach it was enlightening to watch how other faculty members were similarly "guided" to the "correct" answer throughout the rest of the meeting.

Analysis:

Now that Marie is able to identify how others are behaving, it helps her a great deal in navigating conversations. When she is in a potentially conflictual situation or when she begins to become slightly uncomfortable, she takes a step back and becomes an observer rather than a participant. While observing, she has the opportunity to determine how others are behaving. In this case study, she learns rather quickly that the leader of the group is manipulating the group into endorsing a position that he/she believes in. However, by holding a public meeting and inviting key stakeholders, the leader can publically announce consensus was reached by the group. Once Marie discovers this, she has a decision to make. She needs to determine whether or not it is important to her to further the leader's agenda or further her own. If the outcome of the meeting is of little consequence to her, she has very little to lose by furthering the leader's agenda. In this case, it is acceptable for her to be passive and allow herself to be "guided" to the correct answer. This allows the leader to believe he effectively persuaded her. If the purpose of the meeting or the issue being discussed is of extreme importance to her, then she might choose a somewhat resistant approach. It's important for her to be responsible and fair when she is being resistant so she might choose the **Content Process Shift**. Marie might say something like this, "I noticed that you seem to take issue with my observations and I'm wondering if it would facilitate your purpose of this meeting if the group endorsed your perspective outright. Speaking for myself, I'm certainly willing to do that (or I'm unwilling to do that). So maybe in the interest of time we could just agree that's what we're going to do rather than contribute individual perspectives that might differ from that goal." This is a polite way of saying if what you want is my endorsement of your goal then don't waste my time by pretending you're interested in a perspective that is different from yours. Let's just call it what it is and I will either endorse your position or I won't.

Now, obviously, a **Content Process Shift** moves on the continuum to the edge of assertiveness and points in the direction of aggressiveness. This is why the non-verbal behavior and the tone of voice are extremely important when using this technique. Basically, the speaker is saying that rather than discuss the material being presented at the meeting, she's instead going to point out that the process you are using is in reality quite manipulative. By using the **Content Process Shift** it does not put the participant in the discussion of the content, but rather the participant points out the interpersonal dynamics of the exchange. To use another example, if a couple is arguing and they have a personal relationship with one another, not necessarily a professional one, the **Content Process Shift** would sound something like this: "Wait a minute. Listen to us. We are screaming at one another. I don't like the way we're talking to one another. I care about you and I don't want to say something that I will later regret. " The speaker does not argue about the topic being discussed, but rather the speaker points out the method the participants are using to communicate with one another. This can be very powerful because it shifts the discussion to another dimension and it communicates that the relationship, whether it be personal or professional, is just as important as the topic being discussed. By so doing, it can't help but convey mutual respect and keep the participants in the assertive circle.

Take home message: When you start to feel uncomfortable, trust your instinct that you are being manipulated. Step back and decide if you want to let it go or not. If you do not, then tactfully comment on the *process* and do not comment on the content.

CHAPTER 10

Avoiding the Rabbit Hole: Alice's Story

IN THIS CHAPTER WE WILL explore using assertive techniques in personal relationships as opposed to professional relationships.

Alice and her husband Joe had been married for six years. Alice told the group that she often found herself giving Joe the "ice princess" treatment when he ticked her off about something. Occasionally she would go to the other extreme and be verbally aggressive. Neither way felt very good to her-or Joe!

Alice described the time that she asked Joe a question. He just looked at her, rolled his eyes and in a dogmatic, authoritarian tone told her, "I already told you that." She stomped off in pure "ice princess" mode and gave herself some time to think. She needed time to figure out what she was feeling and why she felt that way.

After giving this some thought, she approached Joe and said, "I feel demeaned when you roll your eyes and refuse to answer my question because you are treating me like a bad little girl (**I Feel When Because**)." Joe just looked at Alice in surprise.

"How does that make you feel?" Alice asked him.

"Not so good," he said and proceeded to apologize.

A few days later, Joe and Alice were watching an exciting football game on TV. Joe paused the game to get something to eat from the kitchen. Alice quickly looked to see how the game was progressing on her smartphone. When Joe returned, she slyly announced, "I know how the quarter ends!" Joe was furious.

"Why did you do that?" he demanded.

Alice was initially stunned by the extremity of his reaction and ready to retreat into "ice princess" mode but then she had an idea. "Let me try to step in your shoes," she told Joe.

"Alice, I feel very hurt that you looked ahead at the game score because you ruined my enjoyment of the game *(I Feel When Because)*." Alice said aloud as if she were Joe. She asked him if that statement was correct.

"Yes!" replied Joe after realizing Alice had given his internal feelings a voice.

Alice apologized to Joe and the air was cleared. She figured she was on to something and knew this new tactic would serve her well in the future when communicating with Joe. Although Joe is still not using the *I Feel When Because* statements on his own, he is finding it helpful when Alice uses it for him.

Analysis:

For some people it is easier to be assertive with family members or in personal relationships than at work. For others it is the opposite. Regardless of the setting, we have a tendency to fall into communication habits. Couples who criticize one another, make fun of one another, undermine one another, or fail to support one another can be caught in patterns of aggressive versus aggressive, aggressive versus passive, aggressive versus passive aggressive, and any number of combinations.

When Alice says, "I feel demeaned when you roll your eyes and refuse to answer my question because I perceive that you are treating me like a bad little girl," she is inviting Joe to step into the assertive circle. This allowed him to abandon a prideful response which was then followed by an apology making them both feel validated and therefore respected.

In the second example, Alice's behavior became passive aggressive when she spoiled the game ending. Although it was not intentional, Joe experienced it as hurtful. Joe, who is not accustomed to identifying feelings, let alone articulating them, was able to allow her to "model" for him what it would be like if they both stepped into the assertive circle and responded appropriately. When Alice was able to articulate his feelings and Joe realized how he was feeling, an apology occurred and the air was cleared.

Women are much more comfortable using feeling words and tend to have a larger vocabulary of words to label feelings. For Alice to expect her husband to immediately identify what he is feeling and articulate it would be unrealistic if he follows "typical" male communication patterns (to be discussed in Chapter 13). Based on their past communication patterns, Alice cannot realistically expect Joe to return to the room after she's announced she knows how the quarter ends and hear Joe respond with, "I am angry with you for ruining my anticipation of the outcome of the game. The thrill of watching the game for me is to get in touch with the suspense that builds with every play. You have sabotaged my enjoyment." Instead, Joe responded with a typical male-trained response demanding accountability. "Why did you do that?" he asked.

Some theorists have posed that men are much more comfortable being problem solvers than feeling sorters. If a woman has a feeling that bothers her, she talks about those feelings usually with other females until she feels better. Sometimes, but not all the time, the solution to the problem emerges from these talks. If men have a problem, they tend to mull it over and not share it with others. If they come up with a solution to the problem, they act on the solution. If not then it is easier to deny that there's a problem until they can think of a solution.

A typical scenario of the problem solver versus the feeler is offered by Robert Bly.[1] A wife informs her husband that a male co-worker is incessantly flirting with her at work. Apparently her desk is located close to the water cooler and when the male co-worker passes her desk, he pauses, sits on the edge of her desk, talks with language filled with innuendo or discusses his exploits with other women. This makes her uncomfortable and she complains to her husband about it frequently. Her husband says very little and typically is doing something that otherwise occupies his attention. When the wife questions her husband in an accusing tone and asks him if he even cares if this man is hitting on her, the response is, "Move your desk!"

At this point she explodes in anger because this is not the response she wants and he is baffled. In other words, she wants him to empathize with her feelings much like her girlfriends would. Her girlfriends might say something like, "I can't believe that guy! He is such a jerk!" She is seeking validation and support. She may or may not want the problem solved, but what she most desires is an avenue to express her feelings.

Her husband, on the other hand, who is indeed listening, has stuffed the problem inside himself, is mulling it over and asking himself whether it is a problem that needs to be solved. In other words, how real is the threat to his wife? How much can he do about it without risking aggression? Who has the power to make the coworker stop the undesirable behavior? Is the guy just shooting off his mouth or is his wife in jeopardy? All of these issues need to be addressed before he can articulate a response. In fact, when the wife becomes angry with him because he did not help her "gain emotional closure" he tries once again and says, "Hell! I'll come down there and move the desk myself if you want me to!"

For our purposes, this scenario allows me to make the point that women are more comfortable with *I Feel When Because* statements and *Empathy Sandwich* statements. Women want an opportunity to talk through the problem. Men, on the other hand, are more comfortable with definitive statements yet avoid mentioning the feelings. In this scenario, the husband was trying his best to solve the problem and was ready for action. The reader is invited to view the YouTube video *"It's Not About the Nail"* by Jason Headley to see what the male perspective is like. I once had a male participant in one of my workshops say, "Do you know how frustrating it is to see how the problem could be solved and sit there with your mouth shut and just use feeling statements?"

Returning back to Alice and Joe, after she ruins the ending of the game, Joe comes back with an aggressive statement because he demands accountability. A male assertive response might have been, "Wow spoiler alert! Don't tell me. I want to watch the rest of the game for myself." However, Alice hears the aggressive response, "Why did you do that?" This has the effect of immediately causing Alice to retreat to "ice princess" mode. It has been established in the literature that couples can withstand negative interaction as long as positive interaction occurs at least five times more frequently.[2] So when Joe and Alice communicate what each needs in a responsible way (not an aggressive or passive aggressive way) then a potentially negative interaction can become a positive one.

Take home message: Often, men perceive they must compete to survive and women perceive that they must cooperate to survive.[3] This guides their communication with one another and with the opposite sex. This simple paradigm explains a lot about the ability to move on the assertive continuum and underlines the importance of understanding each other's patterns in order to facilitate a harmonious environment.

References:

1. Bly, Robert. *Iron John: A Book About Men.* Cambridge: De Capo Press, 2004. Print.
2. Gottman, John and Silver, Nan. *The Seven Principles for Making Marriage Work.* Harmony Books, 2015. Print.
3. Tannenbaum, Joe. *Male and Female Realities: Understanding the Opposite Sex.* Candle Publishing Co., 1989. Print.

CHAPTER 11

You Can't Always Get What You Want: Daughter's Story

I AM 41 YEARS OLD and still struggling with developing boundaries with my mother. She exhausts me with her intrusive questions. I am angry and resentful that she must know every single detail of my life in an attempt to make sure her daughter is "okay."

It begins with a text: "Please call us this weekend." I am the introvert who despises talking on the phone and must psyche myself up to dial the numbers to have a conversation. Every week the request continues to appear. Every week I ignore the request. My compromise is texting and emailing to keep her up-to-date. This is acceptable to me since I can pick and choose what I want to answer in a less personal conversation. This was not acceptable to her and continual texts appeared asking me to call. This created guilt and I just resorted to shutting off my phone to avoid the guilt (passive-aggressive behavior).

The holiday approached and I made the effort to call on Thanksgiving.

Just when I think I fulfilled the phone call obligation, the same thing happened the next week. A text of, "Please call us at 7:15 PM Friday night," arrives on my cell phone. I am now being summoned to call and given a time? This cannot go on! I have this ridiculous guilt so I resort to shutting my phone off to avoid seeing texts that elicit this feeling. I tried my hardest to think of how to relate my feelings to her. She despises pedicures so I thought making a comparison would help. Here is the resulting email…

Dear mom,

Please imagine for a moment this is your life. You despise having pedicures because you hate people touching your feet. You have expressed this numerous times to your daughter but she loves to get pedicures and sees this as ample mother and daughter time. Each week she schedules a pedicure for you and calls you with the details of where and when to show up. Sometimes you decline the offer but sometimes you go. You are so crabby because you really hate doing this that you walk away feeling guilty about how you acted. You wish your daughter would see that you do not enjoy a pedicure. You hope she would find other ways to spend time with you. It is not that you do not love her or treasure the relationship it is the activity itself.

Do you get what I am trying to say here?

Please know this email comes with the most loving sincerity and kindness possible.

Sincerely,
Your daughter

I realized she was crossing a personal boundary for me. It seemed unrealistic that I would think making a phone call is a boundary, but when someone is constantly asking you to do something you don't want to do isn't that crossing your boundaries?

This was her response to the email…

So you don't want to talk to us and will never visit us again? Trying to understand

Based on her reply it was obvious that she did not get the point.

I respond as follows…

Neither. I just don't enjoy talking on the phone on a weekly basis. I will text or email you instead. How about if you just let me call when I want to? When I don't want to be on the phone and you ask me continually to call you, I just feel guilty.

She replies with…

Ok, no more expectations on our part. You realize we come from the generation where the voice contact form of sharing was important. Our perspective as parents will always be different from yours as our child. We are putting all aside. Do not force yourself to visit out of guilt. On the hypothetical feet, I would be present with you while you get your pedicures if you so desired.

Love,
Mom

After she sent this she stopped emailing and texting. Silence. I am left in a conundrum of where to go from here? I am feeling scorned and punished as a child would and out of ideas for how to have this conversation.

Analysis:

There is apparently more to this mother/daughter relationship than is presented here. On the surface it appears that daughter is resentful and angry and mother is anxious and needs frequent reassurance as to daughter's intentions to include her. This example is included because it illustrates how the communication skills offered in this book can be useful in reassuring the participant that they are behaving in a way that increases the probability that they will get their own way, however there is no guarantee this approach will work. Using these skills portends that each is attempting to foster mutual trust and respect. It is not a magic wand or a silver bullet. Mother and daughter can use *I Feel When Because* statements and *Empathy Sandwiches* consistently, and still not get what each of them wants. In this case, daughter appears to want distance and total control over when and how communication will occur. Mother appears to want frequent reassurance that daughter is "ok," and that she is not rejecting mother. It might take a trained third party to mediate a compromise if both women decide to develop an identity separate from each other while including the other in her life. Until then, they can increase the probability of "first, do no harm" by adhering to responsible communication patterns.

After having come to this conclusion, to invite her mother into the assertive circle, daughter rehearsed saying something like the following…

"I feel uncomfortable when I am obligated to provide you with information about my life."

"It hurts my feelings when we are not getting along so I would like to find a way to work on this relationship with you."

"I feel obligated when you request that I call at a specific date and time, because I would prefer to call when I can be spontaneous and enthusiastic."

Let's see how this scenario played out….

Daughter played her passive card for a while and procrastinated until she was ready to discuss the situation. She really would like to think the problem was solved but knew if there was never a discussion things would just come full circle as always and her mother would be back to being intrusive and demanding constant communication. She decided to send the following email to her mother…

Dear mom,

*I wanted to say thank you for not pressuring me to call on a weekly basis. You have been very respectful of my wishes. It hurts my feelings when we do not get along because I value our relationship (**I Feel When Because**). You are one of the most important people in my life and I enjoy spending time with you when I can. Sometimes I struggle with the line between being seen as an adult versus a child. There are a lot of decisions and experiences I need to make or have on my own in order to feel independent. For that reason, I feel uncomfortable when I am obligated to provide you with information about my life that I would rather not share (**I Feel When Because**).*

*I am trying to see it from your point of view as well. I do **understand** the mother/child relationship but you are correct that I do not **feel** it as you do because I am not a mother. I need a mother/ daughter adult relationship in my life and I hope we can continue*

to keep the doors of communication open as we move forward
(Empathy Sandwich).

Sincerely,
Daughter

Mother did not respond for a few days. Usually this would instill guilt in daughter and she would regret the email and want to suck it back from cyber space. This was not the case this time. Daughter was not haunted by the spirits of the staircase because she had used her own voice to invite mother into the assertive circle.

Five days later a response came across as follows…

Dear Daughter,

I hope you can stop feeling guilty for things. There is no reason to feel guilt. We have and can agree to disagree on issues. Having no phone communication seems impersonal to me and takes me longer since I continually have to correct my typing. A lot of things come up that I would like to share with you but forget about when we text or e-mail days later. Again, we can agree to disagree.

Love,
Mom

This email helped daughter see things from her point of view and surprise! Daughter even called her that evening.

Take home message: Remember our goal… you may not get what you want when you disagree with another person, but you feel as though you had the opportunity to step into the assertive circle and emerge with self-respect. By stepping into the assertive circle and trying to see the situation from the angle of the other person, each participant gets a boost in their self-confidence and paradoxically the relationship is more likely to be salvaged.

PART THREE:
MYTHS AND MISCONCEPTIONS

CHAPTER 12

Male/Female Communication Patterns – Why This Matters

IN THIS CHAPTER I MUST do something very dangerous! I have to stereotype. Let me explain. Individuals and groups that I have worked with point out that men and women engage in different communication patterns. For purposes of this book we are assuming that regardless of the affirmed gender, assigned gender, or gender identity, individuals will show tendencies to communicate in what has traditionally been assumed to be female communication patterns or male communication patterns. In order to be an effective communicator, at times it will be necessary to show incongruence in communication patterns at work versus home. For example, when I do coaching with women who want to become more effective in the workplace, I teach them how to be more succinct, which is typical of a male communication pattern. When I work with men who want to become more effective in their personal relationships, I teach them to elaborate and use words that identify feelings. (Expressing feelings is typically associated with female trained communicators.)

I grew up in the 1960's in a relatively small, somewhat rural community where everyone in town knew everyone else. Social activities revolved around events at the high school. In this blue-collar town, high school football games were an opportunity to meet-and-greet your neighbors and experience cohesion. Let's

pretend for a moment that it is a crisp, fall night in the Midwest. The
high school stadium is packed. The home team is playing its archrival for
the championship. Both the visitor and the home bleachers are elbow-to-
elbow. Although the air is cool, the night is clear and visibility is crisp. The
fragrance of burning leaves is mixed with grilled hot dogs. The band is
playing the fight song and people rise to their feet in unison when their team
scores. Local college recruiters are in the stands and seniors are especially
excited about their presence. For many of these sons of rubber workers, it's
their best chance for a college education. The opposing team is leading by
only a field goal. The home team has the ball and is in scoring position.
The crowd is on their feet as the team comes out of the huddle. The noise is
deafening and you wonder how the quarterback can be heard as he calls the
play. He steps into the pocket and releases the ball. You can see the spiral
in the stadium lights descending from a perfect arch. The protagonist in
our story, a senior who has had an impressive season, runs his pattern into
the end zone-it's a perfect pass. With arms outstretched the ball appears to
be clearly within his grasp. It seems as though time stands still as the ball
descends in easy alignment with the numbers on his jersey. The noise is
deafening as the crowd prematurely jumps with joy. And then...

He drops it.

The gun sounds, the game is over. Our hero, this seventeen year-old
boy, has dropped the pass that would have won the game. How is he
feeling? Pick from the following:

- shocked
- aghast
- angry
- embarrassed
- disappointed
- devastated
- humiliated
- ashamed
- worried

When I work with groups of men and women and take them through this
guided imagery I've asked them to tell me what the locker room looks like
afterwards. The women typically report that his teammates are surrounding

him telling him not to worry about it and expressing sympathy. The men describe quite a different scene. The locker room is very quiet, except for the slamming of locker doors and the noise of equipment being discarded in a heap. The player who dropped the pass is by himself. He wants to be left alone and the others are more than happy to let him be. It would not be out of the question to picture him putting his fist through a wall and possibly drinking too much later that evening to numb his feelings.

Fast forward to a similar scenario involving a young lady. Say, for example, a senior cheerleader who has always dreamed of being captain of the cheerleaders, tries out in a competition and in the grand finale of her demonstration she does a gymnastic procedure involving a backflip. Her foot slips so the backflip is not executed properly. She loses the coveted prize because of an error on her part, a move that she has practiced hundreds of times. As soon as her rival is announced the winner, the young lady bursts into tears. Her mother, aunts, sisters, and girlfriends immediately rush to her side for comfort. This consolation period extends into the following days and weeks. In contrast to the young man in the football scenario, if his father attempts to comfort him, it might consist of a slap on the back or the offer of an explanation that it's easy to lose a pass in the lights. Little more will be shared between the two men. The lady in this scenario will likely feel the same emotions the football player is feeling. The young lady will however be consoled, hugged, and encouraged to cry.

If you think that we don't take these expectations into adulthood... think again. I've conducted over 2,000 hours of marital therapy. I hear women say, "I want him to comfort me more. When I'm upset about something I don't want him to walk away and leave me alone, but that's exactly when he retreats." This is one of the most prevalent complaints from women, in terms of what they believe is lacking in their relationships with the men they love. While men will say, "If I'm upset about something, I don't want to talk about it. I just need some time to sort it out and she keeps nagging me about it." So when the two are in conflict he believes he is giving her what she wants when he pulls away and gives her space. She perceives that as rejection as if he "doesn't care." This leaves them both vulnerable to misinterpretation and open to an argument, which can escalate into dissolution of the relationship. The authors of *Men and Women, Partners at Work* sum it up this way. The basic survival message for how men and women interact is very different. Women believe they must **relate** to others to survive and men believe they must **compete** with others to survive.[1] Deborah Tannen puts it another way. Women engage in rapport talk, and men engage in report talk. In other words, women strive to establish an interpersonal relationship to build rapport and men are much more comfortable talking about issues or ideas, i.e. report.[2]

What are some other differences that characterize male/female communication patterns? Respected linguist, Robin Lakoff, as quoted in *Psychology Today*, has pointed to distinctive characteristics in women's versus men's verbal communication patterns. Women tend to ask more questions. In contrast, men tend to interrupt, report, or dispute in lieu of asking questions. Women often lead with questions while men lead with statements. Men prefer to discuss the event whereas women will want to discuss the feelings involved. Women are more likely to use upspeak, the tendency to end declarative sentences with a rising pitch. This questioning manner may lead the other party to believe the speaker is unsure of herself and seeking validation. Men rarely are in need of this validation. To the outside world, confident communicators demonstrate expansive body language, a lower vocal tone, and a tendency to speak first in a relaxed manner.[3]

Gender and Non-Verbal Communication

There are also differences in non-verbal communication. The table below notes some differences between males and females. Some differences are dependent on age and culture. Remember that these are basic tendencies and cannot predict individual behavior.

Tendency	Female	Male
Claiming territory	Not as likely to claim a space as their own	More likely to have a room at home (workshop, den) that is off limits to others
Positioning	Tend to stand closer when in conversation	Tend to maintain more physical distance when in conversation

Facial expression	Use more facial expressions to express emotion	Reveal less emotion through facial expressions
Body stance	Tend to take up less space by holding arms close to the body and keeping legs together	Likely to have legs spread apart and arms a slight distance away from the body
Sitting position	Tend to cross legs at the knees or ankles	Sit with legs apart or legs stretched out with ankles crossed
Placement of hands/arms	Play with hair/ clothing or keep hands in their lap	Use sweeping hand and arm gestures

4. www.learningseed.com

Fun Facts in Gender Differences

In a study conducted in 1989, men and women were asked what they would change about the opposite sex if they could. Here are a few items mentioned in the results.[5] As you read this list do you think men and women would answer differently now?

Men said women should...
- Talk less
- Be less emotional and more physical
- Want more sex
- Be less involved with other's problems
- Be more rational
- Put career first
- Spend less time getting ready and paying attention to their clothes
- Stop frequently changing their minds
- Be on time

Women said men should...
- Talk more
- Be less physical and more emotional
- Want less sex

- Care more about others
- Lighten up and have more fun
- Put family first
- Pay more attention to attire and hygiene
- Be more flexible with time

How Do Men Communicate?

Joe Tannenbaum, the author of *Male and Female Realities: Understanding the Opposite Sex*, illustrates female communication mode as it compares to male communication mode. He explains that first men must become aware there is a problem. Issues will not register as a problem unless it is a problem for him. For example, if a woman has a conflict with her sister or her mother, a male doesn't necessarily feel compelled to solve it or have a conversation with her about it. If his female mate has a problem with a guy at work, and the implication is that there could be ramifications at home, then he might be invested in helping to solve the problem. But make no mistake, he would not be interested in talking about the problem just to talk about it. If the problem is indeed his own a number of steps take place before the male will engage in a conversation.

1. They mull
2. They store/stuff
3. They communicate/explode

Mull: A man puts the problem or situation on the back burner. If the problem goes away or gets resolved with the least amount of energy, he wins because men deal with energy as currency. It would have been a waste of time and energy to bother to communicate.

Men are not moved to action unless there is no other alternative. Mulling is not thinking. It can take a few short moments or many years. If the problem is not resolved by the mulling process, the man goes on to the next stage.

Store/Stuff: In spite of the data indicating that it would be to his advantage to communicate, he still believes that it would be easier to keep problems inside. From his perspective he still has control of the situation as long as the problem is within his grasp.

Explode/Communicate: When all else fails, he will communicate. This takes the most amount of energy and is only necessary if mulling and stuffing don't work. This last resort is not comfortable for him. His communication skills are not as developed as a woman's and by admission if he has a problem which he can't solve, it is associated with being out of control.[5]

How Do Women Communicate?

It is important to understand that one of the basic problems in communication is that men believe women have already gone through the same process I just described: mulling, stuffing, and finally communicating, only if she is in trouble and the situation is deemed out of control. In this respect, a woman's communications are perceived as requests for solutions since men don't communicate unless they need help.

This leads to confusion in men when women communicate about an issue. Sometimes women want it resolved, and sometimes they don't. Adding to the frustration on men's parts is that often the women cannot tell them in advance if she wants the issue resolved or not. In other words.... women *express to express*. They are just talking and don't even need an answer but instead just looking for self-expression. In contrast, men are *expressing to resolve*. Remember, by the time they communicate, it is a real problem they want to fix. In express to express mode the woman might be talking simply to keep in touch with the man and does not realize the man is trying to solve her problem. Perhaps it is not even a problem to her at all and she may aggravate the conversation by saying to the man, "Who asked you to fix this?"

According to Tanenbaum, sometimes women have emotions and want to "talk them out" without being able to articulate the reason. Most men (and women who have been trained not to trust their own emotional and spiritual feelings) find this statement almost incomprehensible. There are of course many instances when there is a reason for having the emotion, but the woman may not even be aware of it. Women sometimes find themselves feeling happy or sad for no reason, and they tell men so. Since men always have a reason for their emotions (they may not be aware of the reason, but they know that a reason exists), they tend to ridicule or demean a woman's emotional state, especially if she tells the man that there is no reason for her feeling. As a result of this gap, women have either learned not to talk about their emotions so often or become adept at making up reasons for them to pacify men.

What it all boils down to is that each partner's communication is encoded with a message that says, "I care about you." The invested party must decide if they care enough about each other to decode the unspoken meaning. When women believe that they must relate to others to survive, and they perceive a disconnect, they experience it as rejection in personal relationships, and as dismissive in professional relationships. When men believe they must compete with others to survive, and they hear repetition from a woman, they become overwhelmed. This causes men to take action, and because they are comfortable being competitive, they either dismiss the other party by shutting down or become aggressive. Similarly when men hear hesitancy or a statement delivered in a questioning tone (upspeak), they experience it as an unworthy response.[5]

So what does all of this have to do with increasing your personal and professional effectiveness? If a man wants to improve the quality of the relationship with the women they love, I recommend using attending behaviors more often. This means they learn to listen without feeling a compulsion to fix a problem. They learn to enjoy the emotional connections that a woman experiences when she has a partner who simply listens and supports. Men also need to practice being more comfortable expressing feelings and sharing events that happened while they were away from her. For women who want to be more effective in their relationships, I recommend that they don't make things more complicated than they have to be. Use fewer words to express your needs and wants. Say it once and give him time to mull it over. When men use few attending behaviors and women see an absence of attending behaviors, they tend to believe that men haven't heard them, so they say it again, they say it in a different way, or they say it more loudly. Men can become overwhelmed and perceive this as nagging or condescending. So women, remember to say less and say it once!

Take home message: People can be predominately male trained or female trained communicators. Male trained communicators are efficient in their communication style but run the risk of being perceived as uncaring. Female trained communicators can be collaborative and supportive but run the risk of being overwhelming to the listener.

References:

1. Simons G, Weissman GD. (1990) *Men and Women: Partners at Work.* Los Altos, CA: Crisp Publications, Inc.
2. Tannen D. (1990) *You Just Don't Understand Women and Men in Conversation.* New York, NY: William Morrow & Co., Inc.
3. Kohn A. (1988) Girl Talk, Guy Talk. *Psychology Today,* Feb., 66.
4. Retrieved from http://www.learningseed.com
5. Tanenbaum, J. (1989) *Male and Female Realities: Understanding the Opposite Sex.* Sugar Land, TX: Candle Publishing Company.

CHAPTER 13

Silence is Golden: Lucy's Story

LUCY STARES AT HER BOSS and repeats herself, "So, I just think we need an assistant to get the work done. I am really tired. Bev is working overtime. Deb is missing her son's soccer practice and we are still not making a dent in it."

Boss: "Uh huh… problem is we have a hiring freeze."

"I know that but we are really stressed." Lucy prattles on, " I mean Monday, Wednesday, and Friday I stayed until 6 PM… no wait it was Wednesday, Thursday, and Friday… I think…. Yeah, I remember I was supposed to meet my husband for dinner Friday. No wait it was Thursday. Uhh… Anyway, I am staying late and Bev is about ready to quit and …"

Boss interrupts, "Sorry. No money, honey." Smiling, "Tell you what, if we get that grant we applied for I will take a look at some line items or see if we can justify lending your division a few hours. Ok?" He rises and collects his belongings effectively dismissing her.

Lucy repeats her plea and reports to the others that he is considering adding another person.

Analysis:

Lucy communicated in a traditionally female-trained style. She framed her request for resources based on an emotional appeal. When she did not observe attending behavior on the part of her boss (such as nods, eye contact, and smiles), she repeats herself and absent-mindedly fills in details to make the story more real. Incidentally, no one cares when it was or whatever it was Deb or Lucy missed.

Lucy has a higher probability of getting what she wants if she prepares a **brief** report that contains the facts such as hours worked, overtime paid, and savings incurred if her request is granted. Her initial appeal should be succinct. The short-term memory is approximately five units plus/minus two, so make the first seven words count. It should go something like this.

"Are you aware that your company is losing money every week?" Lucy asks her boss.

Boss: "What do you mean?"

Lucy answers, "You are paying Bev, Deb, and me "X" amount of overtime every week, but I think I have a solution. Would you like to hear it?"

Get his commitment to listen and then present the facts. Then be quiet! Do not fill empty air-time rambling on with irrelevant details. Let him mull and stuff and then ask for agreement.

Lucy proceeds, "Can we agree that we need to hire someone?"

If he says yes, then thank him and ask him to articulate the next steps to make it happen. If he says no, follow up with, "Can we agree that this is a problem that deserves careful consideration and a future conversation?"

Use ***Broken Record*** until he at least agrees to that. Once you have agreement follow with, "Ok I will check with you in a week to see where we are. Is Thursday at 2 PM good for you?" Again, get commitment. Once you agree on a day and time do your homework, prepare your argument, and present it succinctly as many times as it takes.

This approach is likely more effective because the problem is described as one that affects him and not just one that affects Lucy, Deb, and Bev. This moves it up on his list of priorities. Moreover, by keeping her appeal succinct she is not imposing on his time or competing for his attention.

Take home message: Remember female trained communicators can be charming when they tell personal stories in a social setting but can lose the listener in a professional setting. Male trained communicators are more apt to be perceived as on target but can run the risk of being abrupt. Know your audience and present your issue accordingly. It is ok to be quiet and let the listener mull over what you are asking.

CHAPTER 14

Love Me, Love My Dog: Ellen's Story

MARY AND BILL WERE IN there twenties when they initially met through a group of mutual friends. The group spent several years having get-togethers, going to bars, and participating in other social events. At the beginning of their marriage, Bill had a demanding job that required the couple to attend many social events so this became their social life. On an individual basis, Mary enjoyed arts and crafts and Bill enjoyed golf, both on the course and on TV. This pattern continued for many years.

During this time, Mary and Bill had a child. About the time the child went to first grade, Bill changed jobs and no longer kept contact with most of the couple's previous social circle. Since their child was now in school, Mary and Bill spent their social time with their son, his friends, and his friends' parents. Mary still enjoyed arts and crafts and Bill enjoyed watching sports on TV.

Mary and Bill are an example of "when opposites attract." Mary is an outgoing, social, "talk to anyone" type of person. She is creative and enjoys craft projects. Bill, on the other hand, is much more introverted and enjoys relaxing at home. Bill does not seek out social situations but can enjoy them on a limited basis, if invited. Bill has always enjoyed Mary's easiness with social situations and it was part of what attracted Bill to Mary. Mary enjoyed Bill's calmness as she had a tendency to overbook and overwhelm herself with her abundant energy and social desires. Bill's even demeanor helped her to relax. Although their personalities complimented each other, their individual activities did not. Mary was not really enthralled with sports. She grew up in a home where creative endeavors were valued and encouraged. Bill, on the other hand, was not encouraged to pursue creative outlets. In his family, those activities stayed with the females. Bill, on the other hand, had a father who was very interested in sports. He competed with Bill and his brothers in sporting events and sporting events were a major topic for discussion among the males in his family.

Over the years, Mary and Bill tried to combine their individual passions. For years, Mary would bring her arts and crafts to the living room and casually accompany Bill while he was watching golf. Since golf was a slow moving sport, she could mostly listen and look up periodically to follow the leader board. Between shots, the golf commentators would talk, in depth, about the golfers' lives fulfilling the "social" aspects for Mary to relate to the players. Bill also tried to support Mary with her creative endeavors by reviewing what she had made and letting her know which projects he liked best. He also accompanied her on shopping excursions for new craft supplies.

Mary kept looking for ways to connect better with Bill through something in common. Even though they tried other activities, which did not involve sports or arts and crafts, they both really wanted to partake in their preferred hobbies and therefore other events fell short with their enthusiasm.

One day, when Mary was creating a jewelry item in the nearby dining room, her teenage son asked her for some canvas and paint so that he could create a painting. Most of his time was usually consumed with school and other extracurricular activities, so it was unusual for him to have the desire and time to sit near Mary. He casually talked about his ideas for the painting, the colors he was considering, and the techniques he wanted to try. As she listened and watched her son, she realized how much she enjoyed his creative thinking. It really did not matter to her what the actual project was, but it was the entry of her son into her creative world that was so enjoyable. At that point, Mary started to think about her situation with Bill. Mary had less and less interest in his "sports talk" and Bill knew this. Maybe Bill just wanted someone who could enter his sports world just like their son had entered Mary's creative world?

Mary then had an idea. Maybe she could ask Bill which of the two sports he watched on TV were the most meaningful to him. She could learn about these two sports on a level where she could have an invested, meaningful conversation with Bill. In exchange, she wanted designated creative time with Bill. He could pick whatever creative endeavors he chose and join Mary for meaningful time in her creative world. She did not care what creative activities he chose or whether he changed his creative activities every week. They did not even have to work on the same project but they would just be together in her creative world. Mary thought this compromise had a chance since both of them would be exploring outside of their own comfort zone. It would also give them topics of conversation that they would have in common. Bill agreed to the idea.

Analysis:

You need to identify your goal when you are communicating with another person. Know what you want! To do this, ask yourself these questions before engaging in the conversation:

- *Do I want to get my needs met? Teach a lesson? Or pay someone back?* In Mary's situation did she really want her husband to spend time standing in the craft aisle with her or did she just want to spend time with him?
- *How important is the relationship to me?* This is a key point and will determine how much you are willing to invest in the conversation. In Mary's case, I would venture to say her husband is pretty important to her and she would strive to find common ground.
- *Will I accept a compromise?* In Mary's case was she willing to give up the craft idea if another solution was more viable for Bill?

Mary needs to make sure that she is willing to adjust her expectations. In good faith, Bill might make the effort to do a craft project with her but might not commit to doing so on an ongoing basis. After all, she can do a craft (get her needs met) while watching golf but likely he cannot watch golf while paying attention to his craft project. Do you picture men crocheting while they drink a beer with their buddies? They tend to hyperfocus while watching TV and shut out other stimulation making it quite difficult for Bill to craft and watch sports. Is it possible Mary would be just as happy joining a craft group and make a date with her husband to do something else that they both enjoy-say dinner or a movie? She will need to identify what she needs to accomplish by getting him to do a craft with her. Does she just want to spend time with him or is she trying to change him into someone he isn't? In order to answer these questions she will need to use *I Feel When Because* statements and *Empathy Sandwiches*. She will also need to be open to hear alternatives from Bill.

Take home message: If you invite someone into the assertive circle it means mutual respect. You might very well accept a compromise that you hadn't considered before. To determine if you would be satisfied with a compromise, be clear with yourself about what you want and need, and whether your invitation to step into the assertive circle is a veiled attempt to manipulate the other person to give you want you want.

CHAPTER 15

If You Want to Win the Lottery You Have to Buy the Ticket: Suzie's Story

I WAS INFORMED I WOULD be co-chairing a committee with my worst nemesis. I had worked with him before on projects where we were both lead and I had been thrown under bus. It was either that or he would take all the credit never bothering to do any of the work. I swore I would never work with him again. What is one to do though when they receive official notification by the boss that they are to head up a committee with a colleague who they despise working with? I cringed and swore to use this opportunity to practice my assertive skills.

We were assigned to meet with our group over several occasions. On both occasions he failed to show up to the meeting. The group was a bit lost since he had been the one to go to several in-services to establish how we were to approach our assigned task. Since I did not attend these pre-meetings, I was a bit in the dark myself on how to proceed without him. At the first meeting, we did the best we could with what little information we had. When he did not show up to the second meeting, I could feel the frustration of the group come to a boiling point. I tried my best to lead a productive meeting despite the lack of direction from our so-called "leader."

After the second meeting, I sent the following email to our leader.

Hi Doug,

The committee met today and continued our work from the first meeting. You need to provide the group with guiding questions on how to approach our assigned task. Other groups are using this as the stepping-stone for future work. At this point, the group is feeling unsure of the direction we need to take. Your conflicts may be unavoidable but the group thought that if you gave us the questions we could work in your absence and keep you up to date.

Thanks,
Susie

He failed to respond to my email. Alas, two days later an invite appeared in my in-box for a third group meeting. I was annoyed that the group had already met twice and now we were supposed to rearrange our schedules to make it convenient for Doug. I waited a few days before accepting the invitation. I finally gave in and accepted when all other members agreed to make the meeting. At the meeting, he thanked everyone for their hard work and provided direction on how to proceed. I was pleased that he acknowledged the members of the group and their continual efforts.

The next charge on our plate was to formulate a written response detailing the progress our group had made to date. Doug sent me the following email:

Susie,

Let's try to meet, if possible, within the next week to discuss our plan of action. Please feel free to speak with my secretary to find a mutually agreeable time. I am looking forward to working with you on this response.

Thanks,
Doug

I scheduled a meeting through his secretary that was convenient for me. The night before the meeting, I mentally prepared myself swearing I would not agree to write the progress statement. I practiced what I would say out-loud over and over. I was going to take a stand!

After the meeting, I walked away disappointed in myself. I started out by saying, "Since you are the chair of the group I believe it is your responsibility to write the document."

He responded with, "But you are the writer. I am much better at editing."

I replied, "Yes, but you are the one with the background information and you know what our boss is looking for. Therefore, I think you are the one best suited to formulate the response." I was going for broken record here.

The reply from Doug was, "If you write it, I will edit it. I will really owe you on this one."

At that point, I just gave in and agreed to write it. I knew I should have escalated to the next step on the continuum when broken record was not working but I was not fast enough to think of what to do next. I was inflamed and felt like I lost the battle. I tried to placate myself by thinking it might make more sense for me to take the first stab at writing because it was likely he would send me the document hours before it was due and expect me to finalize it. I do not work well under pressure, so I probably saved myself a lot of stress.

A few days later I sent him the document. I waited over two weeks for a reply. He stopped by my office twice to say, "I just don't have time to get to it." In his typical whiny voice, he tells me his life is so busy and no one has as much work as he does. I realized this was his way of eliciting my sympathy and getting me to do his work for him. I was not falling for it this time. When he came to my office to whine I replied, "Well, get to it when you can." This effectively threw the ball back in his court.

Two weeks later he sent the document with his suggestions tracked. In the email he stated the following:

Susie,

Attached are my thoughts based on your initial draft (I tracked changes). Please take a look and let me know your thoughts. We need to have this submitted tomorrow by 8 AM. Thanks again for all your continued support and efforts.

Take care,
Doug

He sent the email at 9 PM on Sunday evening. I made a few comments and sent it back. I was not going to finalize it for him. He would need to do that. I was done. He submitted the document to our boss on time. I was cc'ed on the email but never thanked for my effort. I was irritated. I went to my boss later that day to tell her I had done all of the work. She told me not to worry, as she was keeping track.

I cannot quite decide if I feel good about this encounter or not. In the end, I believe he still got out of the work and tried to take the credit as usual.

Analysis:

Let's assume that Doug is operating from the premise "I must compete to survive." Chances are, he has no ulterior motive. He is simply optimizing his chances of succeeding in as expeditious a manner as possible. It is perfectly logical in a competition to attempt to win. If you can win by spending as few resources as possible (time, effort, money) why wouldn't you?

Women who believe they must relate to survive assume that when a man is in competition mode he is purposely attempting to exploit them. In actuality, he is just doing what he has been trained to do.

When Suzie sends her email requesting guiding questions, she is inadvertently acknowledging the group is dependent on Doug. Doug responded by asking her to set up a meeting with him. Let's review how this played out:

I scheduled a meeting through his secretary that was convenient for me. The night before the meeting, I mentally prepared myself swearing I would not agree to write the progress statement. I practiced what I would say out loud over and over. I was going to take a stand!

After the meeting, I walked away disappointed in myself. I started out by saying, "Since you are the chair of the group I believe it is your responsibility to write the document."

He responded with, "But you are the writer. I am much better at editing."

I replied, "Yes, but you are the one with the background information and you know what our boss is looking for. Therefore, I think you are the one best suited to formulate the response." I was going for broken record here.

The reply from Doug was, "If you write it, I will edit it. I will really owe you on this one."

At that point, I just gave in and agreed to write it. I knew I should have escalated to the next step on the continuum when broken record was not working, but I was not fast enough to think of what to do next. I was inflamed and felt like I lost the battle. I tried to placate myself by thinking it might make more sense for me to take the first stab at writing because it was likely he would send me the document hours before it was due and expect me to finalize it. I do not work well under pressure, so I probably saved myself a lot of stress.

What happened here? First, make sure you know what you want and how you feel before entering into the conversation. If you are angry you may think you are being assertive when in reality you are being aggressive. "You" statements are almost always aggressive. In this case Suzie was aggressive... *"Since **you** are the chair of the group I believe it is **your** responsibility to write the document."* When that got her nowhere she responded with, *"Yes, but **you** are the one with the background information and **you** know what our boss is looking for. Therefore, I think **you** are the one best suited to formulate the response."* Suzie was disturbed after the conversation was over. The spirits were haunting her... *I was inflamed... I lost the battle.* Aggression works in the short-term, not the long-term. Another fair point made at this point is Suzie said she just gave up because she was not fast enough to think on her feet. Practice, practice, practice so that you will know what to say and when to say it.

Two weeks later Doug still had not replied to Suzie. Doug was acting passive-aggressive, yet Suzie assumed he was being defiant in attempting to persuade her to do the work. The final document came back to Suzie weeks later, mere hours before the deadline.

Susie,

Attached are my thoughts based on your initial draft (I tracked changes). Please take a look and let me know your thoughts. We need to have this submitted tomorrow by 8 AM. Thanks again for all your continued support and efforts.

Take care,
Doug

At this point, Susie could use an **Empathy Sandwich.** It would look something like this...

"I appreciate that you put effort into this but I cannot possibly do it justice now at 9 PM on Sunday when the deadline is 8 AM Monday morning."

At this point Susie decides to make her edits on the document but not finalize the changes (passive-aggressive). Doug did submit the document on time to the boss without acknowledging Susie's contributions.

Susie ends with, *"I cannot quite decide if I feel good about this encounter or not. In the end, I believe he still got out of the work and tried to take the credit as usual."*

Yes he did! Doug competed; Susie related. She hoped someone would notice her efforts and acknowledge her work. If you want acknowledgement — do the task from the get-go. Own it, produce it, and stand by it. In other words: lead the meeting when the leader fails to attend, set the goals and agenda, delegate tasks, and provide the finished document. **Sign your** name acknowledging the contribution of others, and submit it to the boss yourself.

If Susie wants to compete and is wedded to the notion that she must relate, then she must confront Doug directly on the issues. She could start with an *I Feel When Because* statement such as... *"I feel wary when you ask me to assist you with a project because in the past it has seemed to me that I do the work, but I don't get the credit."*

Or

Suzie could use the **Empathy Sandwich** which may look something like, *"I know you are really busy, but I am not comfortable making these revisions, so I won't be. I hope you understand."*

Or

Use *fogging*, *"I appreciate the vote of confidence buddy, but I can't guarantee I will have time to do it. Sounds like we both have busy schedules right now."*

Or

A **DESC Script** would apply as well, *"You have asked me to write this before and when I do my name has been left off of the final submission. I would be wiling to write it only if I am included as a partner. If you are not in a position to do that then I am afraid I have to say no."*

If you want to feel ok with how you handled a situation in which you have been treated unfairly, you have to challenge yourself to behave outside of your default position. If you want to reach the cookie on the top shelf you have to get a ladder or at least stretch. If you are afraid of heights, make up your mind to face your fear or decide you are going to live without the cookie. You cannot have it both ways. Doug did not "do" anything to Suzie. He is just being Doug. Apparently this has worked in the past because Susie is pretty amicable. If Susie starts behaving in a way outside of what Doug expects, he is going to have to adjust. If he is competitive then they will have a new understanding of each other.

Note of caution: being assertive can be hazardous to your health. If someone is used to being aggressive and you are typically passive, and suddenly you become assertive, they have the choice to accept that and respect you or they may become more aggressive if they have power over you and they prefer you to be passive. This is why some workers get disciplined by supervisors if leadership is predicated on hierarchy and control.

Take home message: Do not attribute ulterior motive and presumed motivation on the part of others. Choose your behavior based on what is best for you, both in the short-term (the present situation) and the long-term (the nature of the relationship).

PART IV
WRAPPING IT UP

CHAPTER 16

Exorcising the Spirits

OK, SO NOW YOU HAVE AN idea of what to say to chase away the spirits of the staircase, but you may be somewhat disappointed that you're not using these techniques as consistently as you would like. In this chapter we talk about when to use each technique and then we will discuss the barriers to doing so consistently.

So far you have learned the following techniques:

1. I Feel When Because Statement
2. Empathy Sandwich
3. DESC Script
4. Broken Record
5. Content Process Shift
6. Fogging
7. Bared Throat

These seven basic techniques can get you through just about any disagreement or conflictual situation. If used appropriately and consistently, you increase the probability that you will leave the situation feeling good about the way you handled it. You will also increase the likelihood that you just might win the argument, or get your own way. You might be thinking, *I am not sure when to use each of the techniques.* Here's a general rule of thumb. Start with the *I Feel When Because statement.* If you feel too vulnerable sharing feelings, you can use an amorphous phrase. For example, if it's too uncomfortable for you to say, "I feel hurt when you criticize me in front of other people", you might say something like, "It's difficult for me to accept that someone who is my mentor would criticize me in front of coworkers." If you feel vulnerable saying, "I feel angry when you criticize me in front of others", you could try… "It's difficult for me to understand why you would criticize me in front of other people." Note the feelings (hurt and angry) are removed from the second statements. If you are uncomfortable using feeling words, you can't think of a feeling word, or feel as though it is risky to use a feeling word, you can fall back on a few phrases. It might be handy to keep the following phrases in your repertoire: "I'm confused by…", "It's hard for me to understand…", "It's difficult for me to accept…", or "Help me to understand…". Many times these phrases will accomplish the same purpose without putting the speaker at such an emotional risk. By using the phrase, "Help me to understand…" you are asking for assistance, yet insisting in a polite way that the aggressive action on the part of the other person be justified.

Empathy Sandwiches are useful in just about any situation. After all, who doesn't want to believe that they are being heard or listened to? Many times it's the first helpful intervention you can try. An easy introduction to the use of an empathy sandwich is the phrase, "I want to make sure I understand your position." Then you simply summarize how the other person feels or what you perceive the other person has said. You can even make the implicit explicit by stopping at that point and saying, "Do I have it right?" or "Do I understand where you are coming from?" Then you can proceed with your specific request or you can restate your position. It might sound something like this, "I want to make sure I understand your position. Due to recent cuts in the salary level the budget is especially constrained this year. Do I have it right?" When the other person nods in the affirmative, then you add, "I can understand how that would put you in an awkward position. However, as an employee whose workload has doubled, and whose wages have not increased in the last five years, I too am in an awkward position." You see how it works? Now once again it would be important at this point to **SHUT UP**. Do not babble on. Do not repeat what you have just said. Allow your last powerful statement to linger in the air. It is okay if the other person feels uncomfortable or compelled to answer because that is exactly what you are after.

This leads us to the skills of *broken record, fogging,* and *bared throat.* Recall that **Broken record** is simply a commitment on your part to persist in pursuing your goal. If you are meeting with obstinacy or resistance, sometimes it's important to simply alternate an *I Feel When Because* statement with *Empathy Sandwiches* over and over again. Remember to pepper these liberally with awkward moments of silence. This can tell the other person to use the momentum of the conversation to gain some closure. Frequently the other person will meet your request in order to end the conversation.

Fogging is especially useful when communicating with males. So when someone is making fun of you or attempting to embarrass or humiliate you, laugh it off by fogging. Fogging, as you remember, goes something like this: "Yep, that would be me, just a barnacle on the hull of society." The **Content Process Shift** is very similar in that it typically is used as a defensive stance. For example, if someone is making fun of something that you have said, or attempting to aggressively put you down, you simply do not engage in whatever content is being discussed, but rather call them out on the behavior they are displaying. For example, let's assume you are making a presentation and you have cited a particular author of a popular book in support of your position. Immediately you are interrupted by someone who makes fun of the author or the book, or belittles you for citing that particular resource. Rather than engage in an argument as to why that author or book is a legitimate source to be considered, you simply say, "It appears as though you are making fun of me. I question what you hope to accomplish by doing so?" Once again, **SHUT UP**. Let that person stew in their own juices, so to speak.

The **DESC Script** is used when you want to move away from the assertive circle and towards the aggressive end of the spectrum. It is especially effective when you are in a legitimate position of authority such as supervisor/supervisee, parent/child, or customer/business. For example, when a parent is correcting a child's behavior, they might use a *DESC Script* to point out the reward the child will earn for the desired behavior and the consequences that will befall if the child does not behave appropriately. When using a *DESC Script*, never underestimate your personal power. For example, if you are treated poorly in a place of business, using a DESC script and mentioning that if the manager corrects the situation you will continue to patronize his business. If he/she does not, you will give him a poor review on the internet, Angie's list, etc. This can carry a lot of weight. You have to articulate that you are willing to do so and you have to be willing to follow through on those consequences. For example, telling a child that you will throw away all of their toys if they aren't picked up are consequences that you are not going to follow through on. You bought those toys, why would you throw them away? You might say instead, "If you don't pick up your truck, it will go in a box that you cannot reach on the refrigerator until tomorrow." Depending on the child's age, this is very doable and more than likely effective. Similarly, telling the owner of a business, "If you don't promptly refund my money I'll never come back", is not nearly as effective as, "If you refund my money, I will respect your position and speak highly of your willingness to please the customer. If you don't, I have every intention of letting Angie's list and my neighborhood association's newsletter know that you do not value your customer's opinion." In other words, you possess the personal power to engage in positive or negative marketing. Business people who value customer service know this and usually respond accordingly.

When You Get Stuck

Now that we have reviewed the techniques, let's take a look at what stops you from using them. One of the barriers that I hear most often is... *I can't think of what to say* or *I get so caught up in the emotions of the moment that I can't remember these techniques.* If you play a musical instrument you warm up by practicing the scales. If you play a sport, you warm up by practicing the fundamentals. The same is true for communication techniques. If you want to become facile in the use of these techniques you must practice them. For some people, the easiest thing to do is to partner with someone else who is interested in learning these techniques and role-play situations. Ask one another for feedback as to how you came across. If you do not have a willing or available partner, simply practice on your own. Choose a low risk situation and decide that you are going to practice with an ***I Feel When Because*** statement. You can even use a positive situation such as your boss giving you a raise. Respond with, "I am delighted with the award that you have given me, because it signals to me that you appreciate my contribution." Or, when you are with your spouse, try an *Empathy Sandwich.* "Today must have been especially grueling for you honey, what with a crowded schedule and your shipment not coming in on time. I continue to marvel at how you keep all these plates spinning in the air without dropping one of them." In other words, practice these techniques in positive or neutral situations until you can conjure the appropriate words whenever you need them. When you can accomplish this fairly consistently, then you will be able to automatically fall back on these fundamentals when you are emotionally upset.

The next barrier that I hear frequently is... *I get too nervous*, or *I'm afraid I will make someone angry*, or *I don't like to make people uncomfortable*. Psychological literature is replete with information on the importance of mindfulness. Mindfulness is the ability to be aware of how you are feeling in the here and now. When you are anxious your heart rate speeds up, peristalsis slows down, and the blood flows to the gross motor muscles. This is because our ancestors have had to prepare for fight or flight whenever they experienced fear that signifies danger. The important thing to keep in mind is fear is useful because it warns us of imminent danger. Anxiety is not useful because it tricks us into believing that there is imminent danger, when in reality that is not the case. For example, when I am teaching these techniques in a public forum I point out that if I were to announce that I had just received a message that there was a shooter in the building, I could manipulate the audience into hiding under their chairs. They would experience the fear response. Then, if I were to announce that I was just kidding, they would, of course, become furious with me, and rightfully so. But the point that I would be making is, whether the threat is real or perceived, they experience anxiety to the same degree, and in some cases with the same intensity. Therefore, when they are in a situation where they are feeling anxious, they need to simply ask themselves, "Is danger imminent or am I imagining that there is danger?" Unless you are being held at gunpoint, or a dinosaur is about to eat you, there is very low probability that you are in imminent danger. You need to tell yourself that and immediately begin relaxation exercises or breathing exercises so that your body is not tricked into preparing for fight or flight. You want to be clear-headed so that you can choose the techniques you have just learned. You do not want to come out swinging, which is aggressive, or cower in fear, which is passive. There are a number of breathing techniques, mind to mood exercises, and stress reduction or relaxation exercises available. I would like to share with you what works for me.

As you might imagine, I do a lot of public speaking. I am frequently asked if I get nervous or anxious when I face a large audience. The answer is.... Of course I do! When I share this with people close to me they almost always express surprise and say something like... *Well you don't show it!* This is a universal fear and in fact, it is in the top five phobias. Before a speaking engagement, there is a technique I use to calm myself that I typically perform while being introduced because it is completely imperceptible to the audience. It is called Stroebel's Quieting Technique.[1] When I am feeling anxious about a situation I go through the following steps:

1. *Sparkle eyes.* Blink once or twice to make your eyes sparkle. By this I mean look interested. When you look interested people automatically perceive you as interesting. If you have difficulty looking at an audience pick a spot on the wall and stare at that spot. This gives the impression you are addressing the audience.
2. *Sparkle smile.* Smile at the audience. Look friendly, approachable, and warm.
3. *Amused mind, Calm body.* Give yourself permission to be amused by the situation. By this I mean, imagine the audience in their underwear or something like that.
   At the same time remind yourself that no one else knows more about the topic than you. Your physical posture will communicate to the audience that you are confident. Walk to the podium with your ears above your shoulders, shoulders above your hips, eyes sparkly, and mouth smiling.
4. *Breathe.* Prior to rising from your seat plant your feet on the floor and take a deep breath from "the holes on the soles of your feet." In other words, breathe so deeply that you can almost feel your feet tingle. Let your breath out slowly. Relax by allowing your shoulders to slump only for a moment. Steeple your fingers and push your hands into one another. Rise from your chair a half beat from the closing of your introduction. Your audience will perceive that you are pleasant, engaged, and eager to get started. In actuality, you will have tensed and relaxed most of your muscle groups preventing your knees from knocking and your hands from shaking.

This technique is not only useful for presentations but also when preparing to have a conversation with someone who is difficult or with whom you disagree.

After rehearsing and practicing some relaxation techniques, you are now ready to embark on becoming a personally and professionally effective individual who is adequately prepared and comfortable remaining in the assertive circle. What's that? You say there are still barriers? Albert Ellis lists the most common barriers, which they call irrational fears, that people tend to subscribe to which stops them being rational or happy people.[2] Some of the irrational messages we tell ourselves keeps us from acting assertively are listed here:

- Don't make mistakes
- Don't speak or act unless you are sure you are right
- If other people know what you are like they will think less of you or dislike you
- You shouldn't hurt others' feelings
- You should feel guilty if others are upset due to your actions or words
- Pleasing others is better than pleasing yourself
- If you avoid problems or unpleasant situations they will go away
- If you bring unpleasant situations up for discussion this only makes things worse
- What you are worth is reflected by how well you perform

If any of these are familiar to you then they are likely stopping you from stepping into the assertive circle. I invite you to give yourself permission to acknowledge that these fears are irrational. These fears will stop you from becoming the effective person that you know how to be.

What's that you say? But what if these are true? What if I stop pleasing people and they stop liking me? Then what? Then you die? In other words, what awful things will happen if this person stops liking you? Unless you are saying to yourself that if this person stops liking me right here, right now, they will hurt me, therefore I am in physical danger, then choose the behavior that gives you respect not likability. I may like you if you always give in to me. I may like you but not necessarily respect you. Do not confuse likability with respectability. Being likeable does not protect you from the spirits of the staircase. Having self respect does.

There are specific conditions under which passivity and aggression occur which are outlined in the table below. If you cannot identify the barrier outside of you then look inside of you. See if you can identify how you are feeling or what you believe. Do a litmus test to determine if you are being assertive. If you can find your feeling/belief on the table below, it is likely you are not acting assertively, but rather passively or aggressively.

Passivity may occur if...	Aggression may occur if...
You feel guilty	You believe aggressive behavior earns respect
You feel confused or frightened	You have low self-confidence
You are unsure what you want from the situation	You do not want to be seen as passive or frightened
Believing your feelings/desires are not important	You have ignored smaller problems and have pent up feelings about not acting assertively
You want to be liked by everyone	You want to avoid feeling guilty
You believe that a nice person does not show their anger	You are reacting to not getting what you want

We have talked about how to be assertive and when to be assertive so now let's talk about where. You have a right to manipulate your environment. Let's imagine you are being asked to step into your boss' office. You are offered a chair that is too small for you and your boss is standing. You have every right to move to another chair. Similarly, if you're too warm, open a window. If it's too dark, turn on a light. Many times we will not manipulate the environment in a way that is to our advantage and you have every right to do so. In fact, if you need to confront someone, especially a subordinate, you have every right to insist that they meet you on your turf. It's acceptable to set up a neutral environment as well. If you are negotiating with someone, rather than meet in their office or invite them to yours, perhaps the coffee shop is the best place. If you need to have a tough conversation with your mom and you automatically revert to the little girl in your family home, meet her at the bookstore, department store, or local restaurant. Give some thought as to how the environment impacts the message you are trying to impart. Be comfortable selecting an environment that either invites you both to step into the assertive circle or puts you at an advantage.

Power Types

Identifying different power types will help us in deciding where we want our behavior to fall on the spectrum. The relationship and communication that takes place between people is a direct link to the source of power (especially in a professional environment). John French and Bertam Raven are authors of ground-breaking research which was published in their treatise, "The Basis of Social Power".[3] Even though this work was done many years ago, the premise has survived the test of time. Specifically they posed that there are six different sources of power in all organizations. Following is a summary of each different type of power. As you read these over, see if you can identify a person with whom you communicate on a regular basis that fits each power type.

Legitimate Power. In legitimate power, you have power because you are the boss. This type of power is inherent within the position or title. You may be the professor assigning a grade or the boss evaluating employees. Be comfortable with your own authority. Be quick to praise in public and criticize in private. Do not hesitate to use disciplinary action or place workers on performance review. Do not apologize for your legitimate power. If you are uncomfortable with authority, then you do not belong in a supervisory position.

Expert Power. If you are an expert, you are better at doing something than anyone else. This alone gives you power. Make sure that you are using your expert power responsibly. Many times I have seen organizations unwittingly appoint a "sacred cow." In other words, the employee who is the only one who knows the password or who keeps information so contained that it prohibits others from completing required duties when he/she is absent. If you are a manager, make sure that your staff is cross-trained so that there is not just one person who knows a specific job. The expert power should be diffused so that no one person is the only one with the knowledge to move the organization forward.

Reward Power. This type of power comes with being able to reward something when a person performs accordingly. This type of power keeps people motivated. Teachers make good use of this one. Students know that if they behave and turn their homework in they can choose something from the treasure box at the end of the week. Don't underestimate your personal power to reward others with praise, appreciation, or recognition. Think of a time when you have wanted to please a mentor, not because they would reward you with something tangible, but because you respected them and simply wanted to please them.

Coercive Power. This is the opposite of reward power. With this type of power you can force someone to do something. Coercive power is used to withhold rewards or deliver consequences. Think DESC script. For example, let's say you have an issue with your lawn service. You start by saying, "I have asked you repeatedly not to blow trimmings into my mulch. Each time you promised you would do so and yet clearly the problem still exists. I will happily tell others what a good lawn service you are if you comply with my wishes the next time you cut my grass. If I am ignored this time, as I have been in the past, not only will I terminate our contract but I will give you a poor review on Angie's list."

Informational Power. This is one's ability to make things happen because he or she is miserly or they withhold information to make it happen. This is the old sage in the office who knows the culture of the place and has been there forever or the financial advisor who knows how money is allocated. Be careful with this one. Sometimes you can inadvertently have someone with informational power keep the organization stagnant because they are miserly withholding information that causes others to miss deadlines or write incomplete reports.

Referent Power. This type of power refers to your ability to serve as a role model to others. This can also be interpreted as the power that the chief of staff or the secretary has because they have access to the individual who actually makes the decisions.

It is important not to exceed your power base. If at the end of the day the boss's directive is what you will abide by, then it is in your best interest not to be aggressive (or passive-aggressive) with your boss. Say for example, your boss wants you to deliver a message to your subordinates that you do not want to give. Behind closed doors you can be assertive with your boss and explain your rationale. If the boss tells you to do it anyway, you will choose to be passive and comply with the request. You will proceed to tell yourself that you will not be haunted by the spirits of the staircase because you told your boss your rationale and advocated for your staff. You did not have the power (or authority) to implement your plan so you were bound to implement his. Remember there is no value judgment on the type of behavior you choose. It is in your best interest to be passive with your boss to keep your job. However, the boss will see you demonstrate your assertive skills and respect you for them and perhaps more importantly, you will respect yourself.

Conclusion

The queasy stomach, the disturbed sleep, the countless hours of rumination are all familiar signs of anxiety and dread. It is my hope that upon completion of this book, anxiety and dread will occur less often for you. When you are haunted by the spirits of the staircase, you will know that you have temporarily forgotten to use the assertive techniques that you have practiced. The good news is that it is never too late to go back. If you continue to be haunted, I encourage you to do precisely that. Find the person with whom you are entangled and activate a "do over." It can sound as simple as this (*I Feel When Because*): "I've been thinking about our last conversation and I feel unsettled. I believe that we will be able to resolve this conflict in a way that is mutually beneficial. I would like to try." Proceed to alternate your *I Feel When Because* statements and *Empathy Sandwiches* for as long as it takes for the two of you reach a resolution. If no resolution is reached, even after you have consistently exhausted your techniques, then you can conclude that the other person is not interested in staying in the assertive circle with you. At this point, you might consider moving on the continuum to another behavioral technique. Or you might simply say to yourself (or out loud), "This is important information for me to have about our relationship. I will need to think about what I need to do in the future." Then, simply walk away. You may decide to come back, or you may decide that this relationship is untenable and accept the fact that the person will not step into the assertive circle, at least for right now. They may not even have the skills to do so at this point. Regardless, you will feel okay about the way you handled the situation. Which, after all, is our primary goal. This should leave you with a feeling of confidence because you will know that you have the ability to elicit mutually respectful behavior in others, whether or not they choose to accept that. You will know that you have displayed your competence and compassion. You have stayed true to the communication pattern that was most effective for the situation and you will likely be respected by others. Regardless, you will see yourself that way, and ultimately that is the most important step in increasing your personal and professional effectiveness. After all, the primary goal is to accomplish more without changing who you are.

References:

1. Stroebel C. (1982) *The Quieting Reflex.* New York, NY: Putnam Publishing Group.
2. Ellis A. (1994) *Reason and Emotion in Psychotherapy: Comprehensive Method of Treating Human Disturbances.* New York, NY: Citadel Press.
3. French J, Raven B. "The Basis of Social Power," in D. Cartwright, ED; *Studies in Social Power* (Ann Arbor: University of Michigan, 1959), 150-67.

ABOUT THE AUTHOR...

Dixie L. Benshoff, Ph. D., is a licensed psychologist, and a certified teacher who has provided consultation and training for professionals in industry, education, medicine, and non-profit agencies. She graduated from Hiram College Cum Laude. She received her M.Ed. Magna cum Laude from Kent State University and her Ph.D. Summa cum Laude from Kent State University. She also studied at Cambridge University in Cambridge, England. She has been a surveyor for the Commission on Accreditation of Rehabilitation Facilities, and is listed in the National Register of Health Services Providers. She is a Diplomat in the International Association of Behavioral Medicine, Counseling and Psychotherapy, and a former member of the American Psychological Association and clinical member of the American Association for Marriage and Family Therapy.

Dr. Benshoff was the state appointed clinician to serve on her county's mental health and recovery board. Previously she was a Department Director with Akron General Medical Center and the Cleveland Clinic (Main Campus) where she assumed administrative, supervisory, and clinical duties. She has had a successful private practice providing direct care to children, teens, individuals, couples, groups, and families, and has worked in rehabilitation and assisted living facilities. Additionally, she has experience in the public education sector advising administrators, faculty and parents, and providing direct care and diagnostic evaluations for children and adolescents. She has also provided counseling and academic and behavioral testing to the university population and designed training programs for lay and professional populations.

Her areas of expertise include ADHD and learning disabilities, depression, women in management, leadership skills, pain management, increasing personal and professional effectiveness, communication, couple and family counseling, gender communication, and effective teaching and parenting techniques. Dr. Benshoff is the author of several publications. Her chapter, "Female Executives: Getting There and Staying There" is in the textbook *Skills for Effective Human Services Management* by Richard L. Edwards and John A. Yankey.

CPSIA information can be obtained
at www.ICGtesting.com
Printed in the USA
BVHW011400060222
628059BV00003B/17